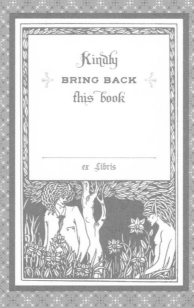

Kindly

BRING BACK

this book

ex libris

DEDICATED TO MY HEROINES:

Marlene, Diana, Isabella, AND *Anya,*
WHOSE BOLDNESS, APPETITES, AND STYLE
HAVE MADE THEM TIMELESS SOURCES OF INSPIRATION.

Library of Congress Cataloging-in-Publication Data is available.

ISBN: 978-0-8118-7413-7

Manufactured in China

DESIGNED BY TRACY SUNRIZE JOHNSON

ILLUSTRATIONS BY GRADY MCFERRIN

10 9 8 7 6 5 4 3 2

Chronicle Books LLC
680 Second Street
San Francisco, CA 94107

WWW.CHRONICLEBOOKS.COM

LET'S·BRING·BACK

An Encyclopedia of

FORGOTTEN-YET-DELIGHTFUL

CHIC, USEFUL, CURIOUS,

and OTHERWISE COMMENDABLE THINGS

from TIMES GONE BY

LESLEY M. M. BLUME

CHRONICLE BOOKS

SAN FRANCISCO

INTRODUCTION

One night, in a bygone era, the Oscar de la Rentas gave a dinner party. And at that party, the following exchange is said to have taken place: Swifty Lazar, famed talent agent, turned to legendary fashion editor Diana Vreeland and told her, "The problem with you, dollface, is that your whole world is nostalgic."

Vreeland's response: "Listen, Swifty, we all have our own ways of making a living, so shut up!"

And then she punched him right in the nose.

· · · ———— · · ·

YOU MIGHT THINK that this was a rather extreme reaction, but if you ask me, it was perfectly justified. For I, like Diana Vreeland, am an incurable nostalgist, and life is difficult for nostalgists these days. "Status updates" have replaced gossiping over cocktails; Starbucks runs have supplanted high tea; synthetic Spanx have taken over where silk corsets left off.

So you can see why nostalgists occasionally have to get violent when it comes to preserving our sepia-drenched outlooks: We're absolutely drowning in Newest, Latest, Faster, and Disposable.

Let's be realistic: No one is immune to the allure of novelty. I enjoy my iPod as much as the next person, and I do write for an online publication—several, in fact—which is an undeniably contemporary occupation. Even Mrs. Vreeland—as she was *always* called—admitted to the advantages of living in the age of penicillin.

Yet the benefits of today's über-connectedness come at a price. Modern living is increasingly about convenience, often leaving behind the pleasures of ornamentation and ceremony. As many of us are discovering, efficiency and quality of life are not necessarily synonymous. New products and diversions whiz through our lives at lightning speed; as we discard older objects and occupations to make room for them, we often don't fully realize what we've given up until it's too late (like the concept of privacy, for example—along with privacy's cousins, mystery and elegance).

An encyclopedia of nostalgia, *Let's Bring Back* celebrates hundreds of discarded or forgotten objects, pastimes, curiosities, recipes, words, architectural works, and personas—some visionary, some deliciously notorious—from bygone eras that should be reintroduced today. The entries are by turns humorous, practical, frivolous, solemn, and whimsical; several have been included solely in the spirit of sheer absurdity. The material draws on a vast array of eras, from ancient times to the Deco-saturated 1920s to the elaborately coiffed 1960s. Not all of the objects mentioned here are extinct, per se, but play a reduced role in our lives after falling out of fashion's favor.

While most of these entries are composed of my own personal appreciations, I have also invited luminaries from various fields to cite something that they believe should be brought back; these include designer Kate Spade, filmmakers James L. Brooks and Nora Ephron, media icons Arianna Huffington and Ted Koppel, interior decorator Jonathan Adler, chef Daniel Boulud, and many other celebrated and accomplished cultural figures. *Let's Bring Back* even includes whispers from Camelot in the form of advice from Letitia Baldrige, Jacqueline Kennedy's White House social secretary and one of America's foremost experts on etiquette.

Before you get the wrong idea, *Let's Bring Back* is not about stopping the clock or extolling the virtues of simpler times. Times have *never* been simple. Nor is *Let's Bring Back* about nostalgia for nostalgia's sake alone. Looking back in this way helps us to become intelligently forward-looking as well. It makes us preservation-minded, astute observers of contemporary culture and helps us evaluate what traditions, heirlooms, and elements of our own lifestyles and households we want to pass on to the next generation. It makes us consider why we value an object or ritual one day and forsake it the next.

At heart, *Let's Bring Back* is a simple appreciation, honoring the history of artful living and artfully lived lives. Each of us hopes to leave a legacy of some sort when we die; yet all legacies—no matter how grand or modest—require an appreciative audience. Even the most astounding legacies can get lost in the dust kicked up by progress if they are not documented and discussed in retrospect.

So let's rediscover some of the things that entertained, awed, scandalized, beautified, satiated, and fascinated people in eras past. From sealing wax and quill pens to the Orient Express, from dumbwaiters to quizzing glasses to the Ziegfeld Follies, there are many delights to be dusted off and enjoyed once again.

"ACQUAINTANCE" Today the word "friend" is used rather carelessly; it should be reserved for the most hallowed of relationships. One rarely hears the word "acquaintance" anymore—a polite, cunning catchall term that strikes the perfect balance between affiliation and distance.

AESOP'S FABLES Although usually considered children's tales, Aesop's fables contain many savvy insights into human nature for adults; they also gave rise to many sayings we still use today. Here is a short list of oft-used Aesop-inspired idioms and the fables from which they originated:

"SOUR GRAPES." From *The Fox and the Grapes*, in which a fox spots a bunch of juicy grapes on a vine but can't leap high enough to reach them. He skulks away, telling himself that the grapes were sure to be sour anyway. Any guy who hasn't gotten the girl probably finds this to be a familiar notion.

"KILLING THE GOLDEN GOOSE." From *The Goose That Laid the Golden Eggs*, in which a couple owns a rather lucratively talented goose. Tired of receiving only one golden egg a day, these gluttons slay the bird and open it up, thinking that they can get the whole stash at once. Instead of gold, they find stinky old innards, like any other goose. The idiom is a metaphor for a short-sighted action that may seem to bring an immediate reward but will more likely have unsavory long-term consequences.

"THE LION'S SHARE." A term from an eponymous fable in which a lion, fox, jackal, and wolf go deer hunting. They kill a stag and divide it into four parts. The lion claims the first quarter because he's the so-called king of the beasts. Then, as the other animals are about to tuck into their deer hocks, the lion takes the second quarter as an arbiter's fee of sorts. Next, he adds the third quarter to his bloody pile to compensate for his part in the chase, and the other animals are left to fight over the last measly bit (although in some versions the lion takes all four quarters). Therefore, "the lion's share" means the largest portion of a whole.

THE AESTHETE Playwright Oscar Wilde personified the aesthete, a dandyish breed of Briton that prioritized the appreciation of beauty above all else. "Art for art's sake" was the aesthete's rallying cry, meaning that art—and lives lived as art—needn't be encumbered with all sorts of pesky, pious moral messages. The *implied* mantra—naughtiness for naughtiness's sake—remains *most* inspiring. Being a nineteenth-century aesthete was a full-time occupation: It required enormous cultivation of wit and wardrobe—and, above all, an acutely appreciative audience.

Society is often dismissive of people who are concerned with appearances, but those lacking an appreciation of beauty are missing the point of being alive in the first place. It's important to appreciate life's ornamentations instead of just obsessing over its drudgeries. As Wilde himself once said, "We are all in the gutter, but some of us are looking at the stars."

AFFECTATIONS Like faux pearls, they become real as you wear them.

AGING NATURALLY Women have likely had some version of nip-and-tuck since the beginning of time, but the results of some of today's "artistry" performed on women of advanced years can be ghoulish. Comedienne Joan Rivers's face, for example, is now stretched tighter than a piano string. She recently boasted to the *New York Times* that she's had so much plastic surgery that "they will donate my body to Tupperware." I also challenge you to read the social pages of the *Palm Beach Post* without shrieking. Nose jobs often age badly; Botox is usually patently obvious (as is shoe-polish-black hair on an eighty-year-old woman). I recently heard about a woman whose botched eye job won't let her eyes close entirely.

One individual who symbolizes the merits of natural aging (or at least natural-*looking* aging) is Carmen Dell'Orefice. Now in her late seventies, with a shock of perfectly groomed silver hair and cut-glass cheekbones, she is often referred to as "the world's oldest working model." Still a catwalker for some of the world's great designers, including John Galliano and Jean Paul Gaultier, Dell'Orefice is definitely what Holly Golightly, the ultimate glamour girl, had in mind when she said: "Wrinkles and bones, white hair and diamonds: I can't wait."

ALL-WHITE ROOMS This might sound "beach house-ish," but an all-white room can be terribly elegant and make its furnishings — and inhabitants — stand out like high art.

One of America's most beautiful all-white rooms is the antebellum White Ballroom at Nottoway Plantation, Louisiana. Nottoway's original owner, John Hampden Randolph, and his wife had seven daughters to marry off to the local gentry and needed all the help they could get in showcasing the girls. They had their ballroom constructed from entirely white materials — including the floor — since light is said to reflect attractively off white surfaces onto female features.

It worked: Five of the seven Randolph sisters were married in the ballroom.

AMBROSIA In ancient Greek mythology, ambrosia was a food or drink of the gods that would give its human consumer ageless immortality. Thousands of years later, the gods saw fit to bestow an earthly version of this offering on the inhabitants of the American South, who served this fruit dish as a transition between the main course and dessert. Apparently, if the cook does not include the coconut, it's not "real" ambrosia.

An 1877 ambrosia recipe from *Buckeye Cookery, and Practical Housekeeping*, by a Mrs. Estelle Woods Wilcox:

AMBROSIA

Six sweet oranges, peeled and sliced (seeds and as much of the core as possible taken out), one pine-apple peeled and sliced (the canned is equally good), and one large cocoa-nut grated; alternate the layers of orange and pine-apple with grated cocoa-nut, and sprinkle pulverized sugar over each layer. Or, use six oranges, six lemons and two cocoa-nuts, or only oranges and cocoa-nuts, prepared as above.

Some recipes call for you to douse this concoction with a wineglass of sherry, put it in the fridge, and serve it cold. Sounds ideal for breakfast, if you ask me.

AMULETS Grisly ones that will genuinely scare bad luck away. One has a hard time believing that mass-produced plastic scarabs or Evil Eye necklaces with Swarovski crystals will do the job.

THE ANDREWS SISTERS Let's not *literally* try to bring them back, voodoo-style; let's just renew our appreciation of them. The original American all-girl band, the Andrews Sisters began touring at an early age. Patty was a blonde, Maxene a brunette, and LaVerne a redhead, so there was something for everyone. After hitting a slow patch, the girls had been about to give up and enroll in secretarial school in their native Minnesota when an orchestra arranger asked the ladies to sing on a radio program. Luck was on their side: A VP at Decca heard the broadcast and signed the sisters to a contract.

TEXT CONTINUES NEXT PAGE ⟫⟫⟫→

The sisters were America's darlings during World War II and for years afterward; by some accounts, they remain the best-selling female vocal group in the history of popular music. Among their many achievements, the Andrews Sisters sold more than 90 million records (they earned nine gold records and were the first all-female group to have a record go platinum), recorded more than 700 songs (46 of which reached the Top Ten on the *Billboard* charts), and were in more than a dozen films.

Today the Andrews Sisters are perhaps most remembered for their recording of "Don't Fence Me In," with Bing Crosby, which grew so popular that many people at the time wanted to adopt it as America's national anthem.

ANIMAL-SHAPED TOPIARIES An elephant topiary in your backyard might be as high maintenance as a real elephant, but it would be well worth the hassle. Topiaries have been falling in and out of fashion since Roman times. I can understand the occasional backlash against the extreme formality of Versailles-style geometric topiary gardens, but the amusing whimsy of animal topiaries should be permanently appreciated.

One sunny afternoon, stop by the Ladew Topiary Gardens in Monkton, Maryland, which sports a wonderful topiary hunt scene, complete with shrubbery horses and riders, dogs, and a fox clearing a hedge; it is one of the most famous and delightful examples of classical topiary in America.

ANSWERING SERVICES Voicemail feels like such a lonely dead end. It would be nice to hear a voice on the other end of the line, even if it's not the one you were hoping to reach. Like your hairdresser, an answering-service girl can be a perfectly adequate substitute shrink when your man isn't taking your calls.

APERITIFS A divine alternative to those vomitously sugar-laden cocktails so popular today. Bright red Campari with a twist; milky, anise-flavored Ricard pastis; Lillet; Dubonnet. The characters of Hemingway novels always seem to be swilling down Pernod in French cafés. Not merely chic and beautiful to look at, certain water- or soda-heavy aperitifs make a good secret weapon for ladies who are light drinkers but don't want to appear as teetotalers. Have you ever noticed how nervous people get around a person who doesn't drink?

APPRENTICES Internships have largely replaced traditional apprentice-ships, in which an employer teaches an apprentice his trade in exchange for the student's continuing labor for an agreed period. The decline of many artisan vocations is going hand in hand with the death of the apprentic-ing arrangement: seamstresses, bespoke shoemakers and cobblers, clock makers, engravers, and upholsterers, among others. I have a London-based friend who brings a suitcase of shoes to a New York City cobbler due to the alleged dearth of good cobblers in Blighty.

Equally rare is the mentor/protégé relationship, which used to be serious stuff. A common complaint about young people today is that they aren't willing to pay dues or learn the ropes, yet many of my younger friends and colleagues have lamented the lack of mentors to give them guidance and advice.

I've often wished that Gandalf the Grey was available for mentoring duties; he always had the right answers.

"ARRIVISTE" A wonderfully nasty yet erudite term for "social climber." The good news: Most social climbers won't know the word and might think that you're actually paying them a compliment, because "arriviste" simply sounds so glamorous.

ART MOVEMENTS The art world used to reinvent itself—and the whole of society—sometimes several times a decade. New movements were constantly emerging: impressionism, post impressionism, expressionism, fauvism, cubism, surrealism, abstract expressionism, dada. The artists who founded these movements took their work and ideas damn seriously and often hated artists from rival movements. A friend recently told me about walking down the street with Pop artist Andy Warhol and running into abstract expressionist Mark Rothko; Rothko turned on his heel and walked away, refusing to acknowledge Warhol. ("He wasn't about to welcome him into the fold," said my friend, herself an artist. "Mark was into serious paint-ing and Andy was just a commercial artist.")

These days, we just get stuck with the nebulous movement known as "con-temporary art."

See also FRONTIERS

[PLATE I]

Animatus Folius

THE ART OF THIS CENTURY GALLERY From 1942 to 1947, Peggy Guggenheim's wildly theatrical, then-ultra revolutionary New York City art gallery awed some and appalled others. The "Surrealist Room" had a black floor and ceiling; frameless (now priceless) paintings stood on baseball bat–like mounts from which the viewer could pivot the work at various angles. Lights switched on and off every few seconds, lighting the paintings at random; once in a while the roaring sound of a passing train would fill the room. In one corridor resided a revolving wheel of paintings by Paul Klee; it automatically went into motion when you stepped through a nearby beam of light. To see works by Marcel Duchamp you squinted through a hole in the wall and turned by hand "a very spidery looking wheel," says Guggenheim in her memoir, *Confessions of an Art Addict.*

On the night of the gallery's opening gala, Guggenheim wore "one of my [Yves] Tanguy ear-rings and one made by [Alexander] Calder, in order to show my impartiality between Surrealist and abstract art." The publicity was overwhelming; while some reporters derisively referred to the gallery as "Coney Island" (due to the "peep show" features), every day hundreds of people gaped at Art of This Century and its groundbreaking inaugural exhibit.

While Guggenheim generally showcased works by established European artists such as Tanguy, Salvador Dalí, Pablo Picasso, and Georges Braque, she also famously championed the works of then-lesser-known American artists; Art of This Century veterans include Jackson Pollock, Mark Rothko, and Willem de Kooning.

Happily, we can still visit the gallery, in a way—it was faithfully re-created for several scenes in the biopic *Pollock.*

ARTISTS' LOFTS In New York City, you used to live in them because you couldn't afford anything else. Now you can only afford them if you are the furthest thing from a starving artist.

ASTAIRE, FRED (1899–1987) Once one of the most elegant and most adored men on the planet. The best homage to Astaire I've seen comes from *Auntie Mame: An Irreverent Escapade*, in which the author and main character, Patrick Dennis, describes the reverence he and his college friends felt for the dancer and movie star:

> Our only god was Fred Astaire. He was everything we wanted to be: smooth, suave, debonair, intelligent, adult, witty, and wise. We saw his pictures over and over, played his records until they were gray and blurred, dressed as much like him as we dared. When any crises came into our young lives, we asked ourselves what Fred Astaire would do and we did likewise.

AT-HOME DOCTOR VISITS À la "Doc" Baker, from *Little House on the Prairie*. There's nothing more demoralizing than sitting in a crowded waiting room when you're not feeling well.

ATTENTION SPANS So lacking these days—and the prognosis for improvement on this front is grim.

AUNTIE MAME This madcap literary heroine of the eponymous 1955 novel remains an emblem of insouciant glamour, the enemy of priggish convention. But once you make Auntie Mame's acquaintance, she makes all of your dinner party guests seem dull in comparison.

THE AUTOMAT In 1902, Horn & Hardart's Automat cafeterias introduced to Americans a "waitress-less restaurant," with huge Art Deco walls of self-serving food vending machines. At the time, it was an exceedingly modern way of eating— *très* Industrial Revolution chic: You dumped a handful of nickels into a slot, and a glass-fronted hatch would pop open, revealing a plate of freshly cooked macaroni and cheese, Boston baked beans, beef and noodles with Burgundy sauce, chicken potpie, or rice pudding ("richly on display like museum pieces," according to Automat devotee Neil Simon).

During the peak of its popularity—from the Great Depression to the postwar years—Automats served "royalty, school kids, the homeless, businessmen, housewives, or showbiz names," according to the owner's descendants;

sometimes the enterprise reportedly sold 72,000 pieces of pie a day. The Automat eventually became a vital part of the era's iconography, along with Babe Ruth, Jack Benny, the Brooklyn Dodgers, and Radio City Music Hall. The last Automat closed in 1991.

An amusing Automat side story: During World War II, interior designer and socialite *grande dame* Elsie de Wolfe—on a strict wartime budget—gave a celebrated dinner at an Automat, in which she covered the restaurant's tables with her own linens, china, and silver; guests, of course, picked their own entrées.

B

BABY BONNETS Soft satin ones in white or pink.

"BACHELOR'S BUTTONS" A far more charming name for cornflowers, which of course have nothing to do with corn at all.

BAGELS

I don't know what happened to bagels. I'm mystified. I sometimes wonder if I'm wrong to remember them as being chewy and tasty and yeasty and sour—as opposed to what they currently are, which is soft and cakey and fluffy and sweet. I almost cannot pinpoint a time when bagels were good, but I'm pretty sure they must have been once, and now they're not. It's sort of like, what sometimes happens with friends—one day you think to yourself, "Were they always like this? And did I not notice? Have they changed? Or have I changed?" Anyway, I wish someone would bring back the chewy, tasty, yeasty, sour bagel.

—*Nora Ephron* • PRODUCER, DIRECTOR, SCREENWRITER, AUTHOR

BAKER, JOSEPHINE (1906–1975) Most people remember Josephine Baker for her famous 1920s dances at the Parisian Folies-Bergère, in which she wore nothing but a string of bananas draped around her famous hips. Thanks to her chocolate-colored skin, Baker was a second-class citizen in her native America—but on the stages of Paris she became the toast of the continent, receiving some 1,500 marriage proposals, according to her official Web site.

A lesser-known fact about this legendary entertainer: She was a dedicated member of the French resistance during World War II. Her undercover work apparently included smuggling secret messages written on her music sheets. The French government eventually awarded her the prestigious Chevalier of the Legion of Honor award for her hard work and dedication.

Angelina Jolie may be taking her cues from history as well: Baker predated Jolie's international adoptive clan by decades. In the '50s, she began to adopt children of different races: a "rainbow tribe" to prove that "children of different ethnicities and religions could still be brothers"; she would adopt twelve children in all. Baker once eloquently stated that

> Surely the day will come when color means nothing more than the skin tone, when religion is seen uniquely as a way to speak one's soul; when birth places have the weight of a throw of the dice and all men are born free, when understanding breeds love and brotherhood.

One of her children—the charmingly rakish Jean-Claude Baker—owns a New York City restaurant, Chez Josephine, which serves as a shrine to his late mother.

BAL MUSETTE A type of boisterous accordion dance hall in Paris, wildly popular in the late 1800s and the first half of the twentieth century. During the interwar years, people flocked there to do the foxtrot and a rather naughty waltzlike dance called the java, in which a man placed his hands on his partner's rump while romping around. French songbird Edith Piaf (1915–1963), who began her career in the bal musettes, paid tribute to the java and bal musettes in one of her best-known songs, "L'Accordéoniste."

Upper-class patrons often lurked around the more louche bal musette establishments as a "slumming it" sort of entertainment; according to one source, some establishments even staged mock police raids to give their customers a cheap thrill. I wish these places were still around; we could still all use a cheap thrill now and then.

BANANAS These days, the primary sort of banana available to American consumers is called the "Cavendish Banana"; apparently we eat as many of them as apples and oranges combined. As much as we like our bananas, our ancestors would have thrown them out the window: Our great-grandparents ate only "Gros Michel" bananas, which were supposed to be sweet and delectable, while our Cavendish variety was practically considered fertilizer. However, in the early 1900s, a killer fungus called Panama disease began to ravage banana plantations, damning the Gros Michel to extinction. The Cavendish somehow managed to brave the blight—and beggars can't be choosers.

However, there may be a time in the not-so-distant future when even the make-do Cavendish may become extinct; Dan Koeppel, author of *Banana: The Fate of the Fruit That Changed the World*, recently warned in an article that "Over the past decade, a new, more virulent strain of Panama disease has begun to spread across the world, and this time the Cavendish is not immune. The fungus is expected to reach Latin America in 5 to 10 years, maybe 20."

Breakfast without bananas? An impossible notion. *Somebody* had better do *something*.

BANCROFT, ANNE (1931–2005) A total fox. Bancroft is perhaps best remembered for her 1967 role in *The Graduate* as the original desperate housewife, Mrs. Robinson; no one has since made misery and boredom look more glamorous.

BANDSTANDS Once an emblem of a joyous community, often placed in the heart of a small town. Equally rare and missed just as much: public park carousels.

BANKHEAD, TALLULAH (1902–1968) Mae West usually gets credit for being Old Hollywood's raunchiest wisecracker, but ole Tallulah Bankhead takes the cake:

   ••• **WHEN ASKED** by gossip columnist Earl Wilson if she had ever been mistaken for a man on the telephone, the husky-voiced actress responded, "No, have you?"

••• **UPON SEEING** a former lover for the first time in years: "I thought I told you to wait in the car."

••• **A FAMOUS QUIP:** "I'll come and make love to you at five o'clock. If I'm late, start without me."

••• **WHEN ASKED** whether she thought a certain male celebrity was a homosexual: "Well, d-d-darling, I really wouldn't know. He's never sucked *my* cock."

••• **AFTER DECLARING** that she never really had a strong interest in making movies, she added that "[t]he only reason I went to Hollywood was to fuck that divine Gary Cooper."

BARBERSHOP SHAVES Although they must have been relaxing and nerve-racking at the same time.

THE BARBIZON HOTEL FOR WOMEN For generations, this New York City hotel was viewed as a safe haven for single young ladies pursuing professional opportunities in a wayward city; men were not allowed above the lobby floor, and strict dress and conduct rules were enforced.

While its rooms were aesthetically more YMCA than the Ritz (small, boxy, one-windowed pink-and-green affairs with just enough space for a bed, a desk, and a dresser), the Barbizon fortress sheltered the maidenhood of glamazons Grace Kelly, Ali MacGraw, Joan Crawford, "Little Edie" Beale, Candice Bergen, and Liza Minnelli (and my own mother, who exported herself from a tiny Midwestern farm town to study piano at Juilliard in the 1960s). Eileen Ford housed her pretty young models there, and the Katherine Gibbs secretarial school's students occupied three floors. There were Barbizon afternoon teas, musical evenings, a swimming pool and a gym, a library, and two lounges "where girls . . . could play Glenn Miller records or backgammon," according to a nostalgic *Time* magazine profile.

Sadly, the Barbizon became a standard hotel in 1981. It has since been largely turned into condos—although a handful of women "living under the old arrangements" are still said to dwell in the building.

THE BARTER SYSTEM Money is too complicated—and scarce—these days.

BATHING CAPS Those bright plastic flower-covered ones from the 1960s always looked so cheerful; they have the added benefit of distracting from the below-the-head bulges and wobbles.

BATHING COSTUME I simply like the idea of getting into a costume to go to the beach or pool; the term "swimming costume" is still used in the United Kingdom, whose citizens seem to relish any opportunity to get into "fancy dress."

BATHTUB GIN STILLS Prohibition-style: much more exotic than a kitty litter box—and they show ingenuity as well.

BEARDS Nicely maintained beards can be elegant on men of *all* ages. Women need all the visual cues they can get to help them distinguish the men from the boys. A note to men: Beards can create the illusion of a firm jawline, which years of fine dining might have conspired to soften.

BEARDSLEY, AUBREY (1872–1898) One of the most controversial and pleasing artists of the Art Nouveau era, whose work is now a connoisseur's delight. Born in Brighton, England, Beardsley didn't have long to scandalize the masses: He died of tuberculosis at the tender age of twenty-five. But before he went to his reward, he left behind an impressive body of unique illustrations and caricatures. Officially associated with Oscar Wilde's coterie of aesthetes after illustrating Wilde's *Salomé* in 1893, Beardsley also created celebrated artwork for Alexander Pope's *Rape of the Lock* (1896) and *The Forty Thieves* (1897).

While many of his pictures were perfectly harmless (Art Nouveau mastheads and borders for books and magazines) or sweetly mythical (featuring the appearance of winged creatures, imps, and satyrs, often bizarrely unrelated in any way to the text), other Beardsley pieces were hilariously vulgar, morbid, or mocking: There were chinless, bare-breasted battle-ax women; corpulent, salacious men; and so on. Yet there was often an undercurrent of humor and even tenderness to his work; he always saw the beauty in strangeness.

See also LITTLE NEMO IN SLUMBERLAND

[PLATE 2]

Young Master Beardsley

BEATON, SIR CECIL (1904–1980) Bookstore shelves and magazine articles are still riddled with Cecil Beaton books, biographies, and references; he seemed to be famous for absolutely *everything*: his illustrations, writings, photographs, costume and set designs, his formidable black book of bon ton acquaintances. While I tend to dislike voraciously social men as a rule, one thing I *would* bring back about Beaton in a *second* are his early fancy-dress, highly staged society portraits, in which he used all sorts of backdrops made from often fantastical materials to surround his subjects.

Look up his 1929 portrait, *Nancy Beaton as a Shooting Star*, in which Nancy is backlit and surrounded by glistening cellophane. Balloons create soapsuds around the "Soapsuds Group" in a 1930 portrait of three society belles at the Living Posters Ball. These might sound like hokey effects, but trust me—they're gorgeous and shimmer with sophistication. Jean Cocteau is photographed surrounded by Beaton-drawn sketches of Cocteau's profile; the Marquesa de Casa Maury's sequined dress blends into a backdrop of the same material. All of these Beaton works were premised on creating a highly theatrical atmosphere and a fantasylike extension of the subject's persona.

BEAUTIFUL TRAIN STATIONS If you were in middle management in hell, your office would look something like the current Penn Station. It's heartbreaking to see images of the earlier Beaux Arts Pennsylvania Station in New York City, with its soaring, arched, glass-ceilinged rotunda and proud, colonnaded facade. It was destroyed in the early 1960s to make way for the hulking, dour Madison Square Garden complex.

Pennsylvania Station isn't the only American train station to suffer the wrecking ball. Other casualties include:

••• **UNION STATION IN MEMPHIS.** A huge 1912 Beaux Arts masterpiece with a magnificent sweeping staircase cascading from the facade to the street. In the '60s, it was demolished to make way for a hideous, windowless postal facility.

••• **CHICAGO'S GRAND CENTRAL STATION.** This gorgeous building—with arched Romanesque entranceways, marble floors, Corinthian columns, stained-glass windows, and a roaring fireplace, was torn down to free up its prime location on the banks of the Illinois River. What's there now? A vacant lot.

Actually, Chicago seems to have an aversion to its historic stations: It also demolished its elaborate 1893 Central Station in the mid-1970s, making way for . . . *ta-da!* Nothing. The site remains undeveloped.

••• SAVANNAH'S UNION STATION. The two Spanish Renaissance towers of this 1902 station became a beloved part of this city's skyline. However, in 1963 the station and much of the surrounding neighborhood was bulldozed to make way for highway feeder ramps.

BEAUTY SPOTS The rather pronounced ones once popular in the French court; they provide a historically minded way to cover up a zit.

"BECOMING" As in: "That color is very becoming on you," or "Rehab clearly becomes you."

BED CURTAINS Velvet ones for winter; sheer white panels for summer.

BED JACKETS Designed for sitting up and dawdling in bed, these jackets are like dressing gowns except they're hip length, so you won't rumple them with your rump. Contemporary ones tend to be made from dumpy fabrics like fleece or down; let's bring back silk and satin tufted ones with a little bit of flair. It would be nice to have one on hand for when you're sick and stuck in bed; everyone feels ugly when they're sick, and a pretty bed jacket improves the mood immeasurably.

fig. 1: CURTAINS ENSURE PRIVACY *and* COMFORT

BEDROOM FIREPLACES Most bedrooms used to have them as a main source of heating; if we ever need to jolt the national birthrate, we should simply reintroduce these romantic features to our abodes.

"THE BEE'S KNEES" Meaning the absolute best. An equally glowing accolade: "You're the cat's meow." Better yet: "The cat's pajamas." No, wait: "You're the duck's quack." The 1920s offered all sorts of delightfully inane animal kingdom compliments.

BERETS They haven't been very popular since Monica Lewinsky sported one during her reign of infamy, but the stylish beret does not deserve to die by her hand. On a more pleasant note, while on a recent jaunt to southern France, I was thrilled to see white-haired old men still wearing them—and they were even *carrying baguettes.*

BERRA, YOGI (B. 1925) Many witticisms have elitist connotations; however, Yogi Berra—who quit school after the eighth grade—remains the king of mensch wit. In case you've forgotten any of his Yogiisms, here's a list of some of his hallowed utterings:

> ••• On why he no longer patronized a popular St. Louis restaurant: "Nobody goes there anymore; it's too crowded."
> ••• "It ain't over 'til it's over."
> ••• "When you come to a fork in the road, take it."
> ••• "It's déjà vu all over again."
> ••• "You can observe a lot by watching."
> ••• "The future ain't what it used to be."
> ••• "If the world were perfect, it wouldn't be."

BIG BAND SMALL TOWN TOURS My mother grew up in a tiny farm town on the Minnesota-Iowa border. One year, big band legend Duke Ellington and his band drove up in buses and played for the town; local amateurs got the once-in-a-lifetime thrill of playing with Duke and his boys. But to bring this phenomenon back, we'd have to bring back small towns (an endangered species) *and* big bands, so we've got our work cut out for us.

BLACK VELVET CHOKERS Perhaps the original "high-low" accessory, black velvet chokers have been worn by royalty, peasants, and prostitutes; they've gone in and out of style for centuries, and there are various theories regarding their origin. Some say that they emerged during the reign of Louis XV; the *beau monde* of that era reportedly adopted the look from the peasantry, with whom they had long been in vogue. However, others claim that the trend began with English Tudor queen Anne Boleyn, who supposedly donned a black velvet neck ribbon to hide an unsightly mole.

In the 1870s, the ribbons became popular again as an unlikely evening-wear accessory; some believe the resurgence of the trend was inspired by a series of ballet paintings by Edgar Degas (such as *The Dance Class*, 1874), in which the dancers sported black chokers. I had always heard that this period's chokers carried slightly risqué connotations, doubling as a symbol of a woman-for-hire; in fact, some sources say that in the late nineteenth century, "ballet girl" was often used as a pejorative term, implying that young ballerinas also moonlighted as *demimondaines*, or courtesans; perhaps this is where the black velvet choker got that particular reputation.

In any case, it's a very simple concept: A slender ribbon circles the throat and is fastened in the back by a small ornament of jewelry or gold, or is simply tied in a little bow. It's an inexpensive, storied way to complement a little black dress and looks especially beautiful on ladies with pale hair.

BLOOMERS If you must loll about in your underwear, don bloomers: those adorable short, poofy ones that just cover *les buttocks*. You'll probably have to have them made, but it'll be worth it. Let's also bring back tennis bloomers, to be worn, of course, under short tennis skirts.

See also MORAN, GERTRUDE "GORGEOUS GUSSIE"

BLOW, ISABELLA (1958–2007) A recent departure—and the world already needs her back desperately. Blow, a British fashion editor and aesthete, was one of the closest personalities our era had to the Surrealist geniuses of yesteryear. She hailed from an aristocratic family whose Latin motto declared: "Nothing Happens by Being Mute"; Blow certainly embodied this sentiment. While working at *Vogue* in the 1980s, she would occasionally trot into the office dressed as a Greek goddess, an Indian maharani, or Joan of Arc (an outfit which included a heavy, oily chain that

TEXT CONTINUES NEXT PAGE ⟫→

she dragged behind her, according to one of Blow's former assistants). A dedicated enemy of convention, she reportedly once wore a pair of antlers covered in a heavy black lace veil for a lunch meeting with the managing director of Condé Nast Publications.

I didn't know her personally, but how I miss her.

BOATERS These flat-topped, brimmed straw hats — so popular for boating and sailing in the nineteenth and early twentieth centuries — evoke images of punts lazily floating down willow-flanked rivers; yet they were also often worn by vaudeville entertainers and supposedly used to be donned by FBI agents as a sort of unofficial uniform. As a modern accessory, they are great-looking in any context — on men or women — especially tipped forward over one's forehead.

Designer Marc Jacobs featured some rather disheveled-looking ones in a recent collection, but at $400 a pop, they didn't exactly create a mainstream furor.

BOGART, HUMPHREY (1899–1957) When I asked a girlfriend of mine what she'd most like to bring back, she looked at me squarely and said, "Men who drink whisky and smoke." Which, of course, sounded to me like we needed to pay a little homage to actor Humphrey Bogart here; after all, according to one account, his last words were, "I should never have switched from scotch to martinis."

Bogart played characters who balanced *machismo* with tenderness and inner nobility — such an attractive formula that someone should figure out how to bottle it.

BOHEMIAN GREENWICH VILLAGE Once the cradle of American counterculture, today the Village is all maternity-clothes stores and Starbucks; there's a Sunglass Hut on Bleecker Street, for God's sake.

BOOKS How can one read such classics as *The House of Mirth* on a screen? It seems unnatural. While they may be convenient, today's electronic readers are tomorrow's junk; they will inevitably become broken or outmoded, like all of our other technological gadgets.

fig. 2: A STACK OF BOOKS MAKES A SWELL SIDE TABLE

Books are like hallowed old friends, always on hand to inspire, console, or amuse. I'm an incorrigible underliner; I also fold down the corners of pages containing meaningful passages. As a result, some of my favorite books resemble accordions. Years ago, I began recording where and when I had read each book on the inside of its front cover; for example, *Nancy Cunard: Heiress, Muse, Political Idealist* was read on my honeymoon; *The Sheltering Sky* was read while I traveled through Morocco; *D.V.* was first read on the beach in Dubai. Taking these books off the shelves and reading the inscriptions takes me back to these evocative journeys in a way that a soulless electronic reader never could.

BOOKPLATES When you buy an old book, the original owner's bookplate in the front of the book tells its own short story; therefore, you're getting two stories for the price of one.

BOOK SLIPCOVERS Books used to be considered treasured household objects, and great pains were taken to care for them. Many books came with beautiful fitted cardboard slipcovers; in their absence, people would create their own from scraps of wallpaper or wrapping paper.

BONBONS While many types of candy today are alluded to as "bonbons," the cream-in-the-middle chocolate version of this confection used to be the symbol of glamorous indolence; a lady of leisure would supposedly lie in bed all day and eat bonbons. In the popular imagination, these ladies were, of course, invariably clad in marabou-fringed dressing gowns.

"BON TON" A rather old-fashioned term meaning "fashionable society," most frequently used in sentences such as: "These days, she's been swanning about with the *bon ton*, with hardly a thought for her old friends and associates."

BOUDOIRS Along with home libraries, one of the most glaring, lifestyle-altering, meanest omissions from modern houses.

BOWLES, SALLY The title character and heroine of Christopher Isherwood's famous short story "Sally Bowles" later inspired the film and play *Cabaret*. Scandalously liberated, naughty, and a haver of countless affairs, Sally was a 1930s predecessor to *Breakfast at Tiffany*'s Holly Golightly. Critics of *Tiffany's* author Truman Capote haven't always been charitable about the homage; at least one of Capote's contemporaries accused him of brazenly ripping off Miss Bowles. Wherever your sympathies fall in this debate, any fan of Holly Golightly would equally enjoy the tragicomical adventures of Miss Bowles as well; *do* look her up.

BOWS AND CURTSIES These are especially appealing when practiced by children, who these days are more likely to greet adults with a sullen shrug than a polite salutation.

BRAIDS Not just for Heidi and Gretel anymore, braids recently reemerged for a few seasons on runways, in magazine editorials, and on a few fashionable young creatures in New York City and Los Angeles, although the trend seems to be petering out again. Braids can look very modern and even edgy; they are a practical and easy alternative to the laborious drying of one's hair to perfection every morning. When wound in a fashionable twist at the nape of one's neck, they can look like elaborately wrought works of art.

BREAD Ever since trend diets declared bread the enemy, eating it has become akin to visiting a beloved friend in prison. I eagerly await bread's parole.

BRICE, FANNY (1891–1951) Launched on the stages of vaudeville, Brice is considered by many to be the original queen of comedy in America. Famous for her parodies (she spoofed ballerinas, opera singers, movie vamps, child stars, and nudists, among other susceptible creatures), Brice once reportedly described herself as "a cartoonist working in the flesh." Her forty-year career paved the way for other female comediennes like Lucille Ball, Carole Burnett, and Gilda Radner.

Like lesser mortals, she couldn't please everyone all of the time. When Brice—whose Yiddish accent and persona formed the cornerstone of her success—decided to have cosmetic surgery on her nose, theater critic Dorothy Parker sniped that Brice had "cut off her nose to spite her race."

Yet many Americans considered her a great national treasure; in addition to being a brilliant clown and satirist, Brice came to symbolize the fulfilled American dream to her contemporaries, especially to second-generation immigrants like herself.

BRIDGE This one comes at the request of my husband, who's bored to sobs of poker. Along with Bridge, let's bring back Spades, Hearts, and Rummy as well. My grandfather used to play Pinochle with the other men on the train home from work.

THE BRINKLEY GIRLS In the 1920s, the flapper became the symbol of the newly liberated woman, who cropped her hair, wore makeup, stayed out dancing all night, and smoked to her heart's content. And the "Brinkley Girls"—stars of a wildly popular, beautifully illustrated adult-cartoon by artist Nell Brinkley—came to embody the glamour of the flapper; they were "bright-eyed and laughing with cupid's bow lips and innocent sexuality, their fashionable clothing swirling revealingly around their bodies," according to Trina Robbins, who edited a book on Brinkley's drawings.

The Brinkley Girls were more mistress than feminist, despite their self-emancipation from Victorian primness; they were always wheedling diamond bracelets, diamond-covered turbans, and generally diamond-covered *everything* out of their suitors and sugar daddies. In any case, the serials provide a fascinating window into glamorized flapper culture.

TEXT CONTINUES NEXT PAGE ⟫→

Several different Brinkley Girls serials ran over the years in the *American Weekly*, under titles such as "The Lure of the American Golden Girl," "The Adventures of Prudence Prim," and "The Fortunes of Flossie," who was introduced to readers with the following verses:

> *NOW, Flossie was a flapper of the up-to-datest sort;*
> *She was long on looks and money, though her hair and skirts were short.*
> *And Flossie was a charmer, and Flossie was a blonde,*
> *So gentlemen preferred her, and waxed exceedingly fond.*
>
> *MISS FLOSSIE loved excitement, and she loved the passing show;*
> *And she loved to go to places where she hadn't ought to go.*
> *She adored the giddy night clubs and the jazzy cabarets,*
> *She loved to turn days into nights and turn nights into days.*

BROOCHES "In" one season and "out" the next, brooches can be delightful and should always have a place in our jewelry boxes. If you need inspiration, look up the Duchess of Windsor's famous, whimsical collection of Cartier-designed bejeweled animal brooches, including her "duck's profile" pin, flamingo pin, and panther brooch (the animal's body was covered with 106 sapphires and had diamonds for spots—it was also perched on a 152-carat sapphire). Fortunately, this collection has spawned a thousand inexpensive imitations, so you don't have to marry an abdicating king to score one.

BROWN-PAPER-AND-TWINE WRAPPED PACKAGES Fräulein Maria loved them in *The Sound of Music*, and so do I. They are a democratic approach to gift wrapping—and terribly mysterious as well. There could be anything from a diamond necklace to a slab of fish inside.

BUSTLES A good way to hide a large derrière; people will just attribute its size to the bustle.

BUTLERS They provide the household with an air of refinement, so you don't have to.

BUTLER'S PANTRIES Popular in the nineteenth and early twentieth centuries, butler's pantries—also called china pantries—were small rooms built in between the dining room and kitchen. Used mostly to house extra dishes, linens, and dried and canned foodstuffs, butler's pantries also occasionally stored silver and fine china; in some elite European manor homes, it is said that butlers often slept in the pantry to keep a watchful eye over the silver.

My childhood home had a butler's pantry with a swinging door to the dining room, which caused all sorts of amusingly disastrous accidents as food was carried into and out of the kitchen.

BUTTER Especially at restaurants, which usually provide a sloshing bog of stringent olive oil with your bread basket these days. Pats of butter are much more pleasing to behold, especially when restaurants mold them into pretty shapes.

fig. 3: FAT IS FLAVOR

BUTTONHOLE LAPEL FLOWERS They look confident and lovely. Some men might worry that the look is too effeminate, and that's too bad for them. These are the same men who would shy away from pink or lavender shirts, which are considered by menswear experts to be the most flattering shades for nearly all complexions.

C

CABLE CARS Once operated in many major American cities, the sole elaborate cable car system left today is in San Francisco, where it is a hallowed part of residents' lives. America's most famous streetcar (a close cousin to the cable car) is, of course, named Desire; it ran on a route through New Orleans' famed French Quarter on Royal and Bourbon Streets and was immortalized by Tennessee Williams' 1947 play. Also called No. 952, this car appeared to be doomed to the dustheap when it was given a second life in San Francisco, where it still delights tourists and locals alike.

fig. 4: CABLE CARS:
STYLISH *and* PRACTICAL

CAFÉ SOCIETY Until the twentieth century, elite entertaining and frolicking used to take place behind closed doors in the form of at-home teas, luncheons, dinners, and balls. However, as hotel lobbies, restaurants, nightclubs, and cafés gained popularity, "café society" evolved as a term to describe the glamorous new set of people who now indulged in more public diversions. The term was especially popular after the end of Prohibition (which literally drove entertaining underground in many cases), when the denizens of café society flocked to New York City's semiprivate supper clubs such as El Morocco, the Stork Club, and the '21' Club. The rise of photo-journalism and then the paparazzi made café society members even more visible to the masses, through the pages of gossip glossies and columns.

The term fell out of use when *jet set* came along and shoved it off the stage.

CAFTANS Those old society girls in the 1960s and '70s were on to something: Their caftans reeked of "Yves Saint Laurent in Marrakech" glamour, yet they are *very* forgiving garments. It would be lovely to have these robe-like dresses back, as a chaser to the punishing recent reign of skinny jeans.

CALLING CARDS In Victorian times, calling cards were an absolute social necessity. They became an inspired art form, and like so many Victorian objects, they had their own coded language. The folding of card corners communicated different meanings; for example, if you were making an I'm-leaving-on-a-long-trip-and-came-to-say-goodbye visit, you would tuck down the lower right-hand corner. Sometimes gentlemen callers would inscribe initials upon the card to denote the reason for their visit:

P. F. – Congratulations *(pour féliciter)*

P. R. – Thank you *(pour remercier)*

P. C. – Condolences *(pour condoléance)*

P. F. N. A. – Happy New Year *(pour féliciter Nouvel An)*

P. P. C. – Taking leave *(pour prendre congé)*

P. P. – Introducing yourself *(pour présenter)*

Once a man married, he would send new calling cards to those friends and acquaintances deemed respectable enough to visit his new marital nest (anyone who'd accompanied him on too many premarital debauches could likely expect not to receive one). Married men had bigger calling cards than bachelors; ladies were generally given calling cards of their own a year after making their debuts.

Let's start using a modernized version of the calling card as an alternative to dispensing grim-colored business cards at parties. There's nothing more off-putting than someone who relentlessly mixes business with pleasure.

See also FANS, HANDHELD *and* THE LANGUAGE OF FLOWERS

THE CANCAN All the rage in the 1800s, it's always most exciting to audiences when performed *sans* knickers.

CANDLE CHANDELIERS No artificial light can flatter a room—or its inhabitants—the way a candlelit chandelier does. This fact makes the risk of being pelted with melting wax entirely worth it.

CANDLELIT CHRISTMAS TREES Not that Christmas-tree lights aren't pretty, but actual candles make a tree look holy.

See also IMPRACTICALITY

fig. 5: O TANNENBAUM

CANDY-STRIPED BARBERSHOP POLES My childhood bowl-cut hairstyle was administered in a barbershop; the presence of a big twirling peppermint stick outside made the experience less traumatizing.

THE CANTERBURY TALES Fifteenth-century toilet humor: The word *fart* appears rather liberally throughout. I'm personally partial to "The Summoner's Tale," in which the main character, Thomas, who's ill in bed, tells an annoying, solicitous visiting friar to reach underneath him to find a gift of money. While the greasy friar is groping around in the bed, Thomas lets out a terrifically noisy fart.

CAR TAIL FINS First created to house taillights in 1948 by General Motors, the car tail fin shape was inspired by World War II P-38 fighter airplanes; yet by the late '50s, Cadillacs began to resemble rockets more than planes. Sheerly decorative, tail fins acquired increasingly wild proportions (a 1959 model sported exaggerated "batwings," according to one automotive historian) until the trend died out; until it did, fins became the symbol of the midcentury American car.

Hopefully someone will invent a fuel-efficient, tail-finned convertible, one in which you could jet around wearing big sunglasses and a billowing headscarf.

CARD CATALOGS IN LIBRARIES Admittedly, it was nearly impossible to find the book you were actually looking for, but in the process of digging through the drawers, you always came across wonderful random titles that you'd never have discovered otherwise.

THE CAROL BURNETT SHOW One of my biggest childhood treats was being allowed to stay up late enough to watch reruns of *The Carol Burnett Show*, a comedy variety show that won heaps of Emmys following its 1967 debut. Famous sketches included:

- • • "AS THE STOMACH TURNS," ridiculing the soap opera *As the World Turns*
- • • "WENT WITH THE WIND," a parody of *Gone with the Wind*, including a scene with Burnett as Scarlett O'Hara in a window-curtain dress—complete with the curtain rod
- • • "MR. TUDBALL AND MRS. WIGGINS," in which Burnett plays the most hilariously stupid secretary alive; Mr. Tudball, her toupee-wearing boss, was always trying hopelessly to teach Mrs. Wiggins how to use the office intercom, the buzzer, and other complicated technologies

I also love Carol Burnett for her now-obscure children's book, *What I Want to Be When I Grow Up* (1975), featuring photographs of Burnett amusingly costumed in the garb of a variety of professions, including a trapeze artist, rock singer, miner, karate instructor, pilot, and lifeguard. A product of second-wave feminism, the book's final page features Burnett standing behind a podium bearing the presidential seal; the text reads: "Someday I might even be president." In the introduction, Burnett reveals to her young readers the secret behind her success:

> If you asked anyone at that time if a woman could succeed . . . , the answer was no . . . But—and here's the trick—I didn't ask anyone else. I did it myself because I wanted to do it, even if it was the most unlikely, outrageous and insane thing to do. I worked hard—and *it* worked!

If you can find the book these days, it's as evocative a window into the era as the 1972 album *Free to Be . . . You and Me*.

CASTLE HOUSES These wittily named affairs were neither castles nor houses; they were dance clubs set up by famed ballroom dancers Irene and Vernon Castle, who popularized the fox-trot and introduced the tango to Americans at the establishments. The Anti-Saloon League came out against the Castles and these risqué new dances; the "old order" objected to the tango in particular because it was 1) *terribly* risqué, and 2) even worse, foreign.

Yet many leading New York City–based socialites of the day, including Mrs. Stuyvesant Fish and Mrs. Rockefeller, threw their legitimizing support behind the Castles.

The original Castle House was located across the street from the Ritz-Carlton Hotel and included several separate mirror-lined ballrooms for different types of dancing. The Castles taught New York society the latest dance steps by day, and played host and performed at their club and its café by night. The couple soon opened up "Castles-by-the-Sea" in Long Beach, Long Island, and then a nightclub, "Castles-in-the-Air," on top of the Forty-Fourth Street Theater.

The fun ended with World War I; Vernon was killed in 1918. The Castles' rise to fame and fortune was immortalized in *The Story of Vernon and Irene Castle* (1939), starring Fred Astaire and Ginger Rogers.

CBGB Launched in 1973, this now-extinct punk-rock club mecca in Manhattan's Bowery neighborhood launched or hosted most, if not all, of the punk and punk-influenced giants, including the Ramones, the Misfits, the Patti Smith Group, Blondie, and the Talking Heads. After closing in 2006, CBGB became a John Varvatos clothing store; the legacy-minded Varvatos saw fit to preserve the graffiti-covered walls of what *New York* magazine once called "the most godforsaken bathroom in Christendom."

Other similarly filthy dives remain, but once in a while you crave the real thing.

THE CEDAR TAVERN Another storied Manhattan dump, the Cedar Tavern occupied several locations throughout its history, but its heyday took place at 24 University Place, where it became the 1950s hangout for a rowdy crowd of prominent Abstract Expressionist painters and Beat writers, including Jackson Pollock, Willem de Kooning, Mark Rothko, Franz Kline, Allen Ginsberg, Jack Kerouac, Frank O'Hara, and LeRoi Jones.

The Tavern's most celebrated patron, Pollock, was reportedly banned after ripping the men's room door from its hinges; ditto for Kerouac, who allegedly peed in an ashtray. The neighborhood was dangerous, muggings were common, and the early allure of the Tavern appears to have been its cheap alcohol; still, historians consider it an important incubator of the now-iconic Abstract Expressionist movement. When this location was demolished in the '60s, Cedar Tavern moved up the street, but the scene was never the same; the later incarnation of the bar closed in 2006.

CENTER PARTS They have the curious effect of making one's features appear slightly asymmetrical and therefore bring out what is unique about each face.

CHALKBOARD BILLS IN RESTAURANTS The old-fashioned bistro ritual of presenting your bill chalked onto a slate board is actually rather forward looking and preservation-minded: It saves paper.

CHAMPAGNE-GLASS TOWERS A round pyramid of stacked coupe champagne glasses, in which champagne is poured into the top glass and eventually trickles down to the ones on the lower tiers. Popular in the 1920s, such towers are the prettiest monuments to decadence.

CHAMPAGNE JELLY MOLDS There really should be an infinite number of ways to enjoy champagne. Perhaps we should use it as perfume too: a dab on each wrist and behind each ear.

CHARGERS Especially silver or silver-plated ones. You can use these decorative "under-plate" platters for a dinner party when you don't have time to iron a tablecloth; they lend instant formality. I don't know why chargers went out of style; but then again, in some circles, *underpants* are out of fashion these days, so go figure.

CHARIOTS The ultimate status vehicle, especially when drawn by lions or elephants.

CHARM SCHOOL Let's be honest: We all know a person or two who could really use it.

CHASSEURS "Runners" at elite restaurants such as Maxim's in Paris. If you needed anything during your meal, like cigarettes or a copy of the evening newspapers, a chasseur would scramble out and get it for you. Although these days, given our dearth of evening newspapers and one's inability to smoke in restaurants, it's unclear what you'd send a chasseur out to fetch: perhaps a copy of an old-fashioned title like the *New Yorker* or *Vanity Fair*, or a racing publication, just to stay in the spirit of the old days.

CHECKERED YELLOW CABS A barely detectable ribbon of checkers adorns the backs of current New York taxis; I can't imagine why on *earth* one of the most memorable emblems of New York City was abolished in this thoughtless manner. But on the bright side, at least the cabs are still yellow.

CHEERLEADERS Of a quainter variety, as opposed to today's absolutely violent ones, who look like backup dancers for a Britney Spears video.

CHICKEN PAILLARD And other such Jackie Kennedy–era culinary favorites, like Waldorf Salad and Duck a l'Orange.

Note the old-fashioned delectables on this menu from a Jacqueline Kennedy White House Luncheon, given on April 11, 1961, for the Ladies of the Press:

Seafood Newberg

Hungarian goulash with noodles

Cold turkey

Ham and tongue in chaud-froid

Cold poached salmon with green sauce

Galantine of veal

Pictures of Kennedy White House formal table settings are fascinating: The flower arrangements—often long-stemmed roses mixed with country flowers—are so specific to the aesthetics of that era. Little gold or silver cups of cigarettes also sat at each setting.

CHIMNEY SWEEPS In parts of Great Britain it is considered lucky for a bride to see a chimney sweep on her wedding day. And apparently you get even *more* good luck if you see the chimney sweep's brush popping out of the top of a chimney on the way to the church. This is reason enough to bring "sweeps" back in spades: With a fifty percent divorce rate in America, young couples need all the luck they can get.

CHUBBIES These wonderful short fur jackets were must-haves for any fashion-minded midcentury woman. One advantage: They're literally so chubby that they make the rest of you look very svelte by comparison.

CHUCKLES Chuckles jelly candies—first introduced by Farley's & Sathers Candy Company in 1921—used to be a vending-machine and five-and-dime store favorite, but they're getting hard to find now. Each package contains a rather radioactive rainbow of lime, licorice, lemon, cherry, and orange sugar-coated jellies. In my family, there was always a fight over who got saddled with the black licorice piece: Usually it was me, and as a result, I've come to crave them.

CHUMLEY'S A pub, 1920s speakeasy, and cultural landmark in New York City's Greenwich Village, Chumley's was a gathering place for writers, poets, journalists, and activists of the Lost Generation, the Beat Generation, and all sorts of other generations. Located at 86 Bedford Street, it once sported a "secret" entrance on Barrow Street with no exterior sign. According to at least one source, the address gave rise to the expression "to 86" (meaning to hide or get rid of something, or to stop serving a person). Right before Prohibition agent raids, paid police sources would call the Chumley's staff and warn them to "86 everyone out the back door."

In more recent years, the food at Chumley's could be a little questionable, but its walls were covered with wonderful yellowing photos of its famous historical patrons; a lazy old dog often roved among the tables; and a fire

TEXT CONTINUES NEXT PAGE ⟫→

roared in the front-room fireplace. Then, shockingly, the building partially collapsed in 2007 and was subsequently torn down, erasing nearly a century of history.

The pub had been a favorite destination for sailors during New York City's annual Fleet Week; today it's sad to see the men in white uniforms—who haven't yet heard the news of the bar's demise—wandering the neighborhood, not knowing that they're looking for a ghost.

CIGARETTE CASES A wonderful way to carry your new calling cards.

CIGARETTE GIRLS Cockatoos in hot pants.

CIRCULAR SOFAS An elegant Victorian furnishing for givers of serious parties; guests perched on straight couches always have that "crow on a wire" look.

THE CLAREMONT RIDING ACADEMY Built in 1892, Claremont was a wonderful, rickety old stable and riding academy that lived right smack in the middle of Manhattan's Upper West Side. It had been a multistory stable; I always liked the idea of horses living in an apartment building, like everyone else in New York, having busy luncheon schedules and dance cards.

Claremont closed its doors in 2007; it had been the oldest continuously operated equestrian stable in New York City. Horseback riding in Central Park—once one of the city's more romantic ways to spend an autumn afternoon—is now largely a fabled, extinct pastime.

CLAMBAKES By some accounts, American clambakes originated with the earliest European settlers to New England, who learned the art of cooking crustaceans in a beach sandpit from the local Native Americans. They became extremely popular with the rise of beach culture in the twentieth century, although they're often deemed too inconvenient for today's grill-addicted outdoor chefs.

For those disinclined to cook dinner in a hole in the ground, chef Ina Garten—a.k.a. "The Barefoot Contessa"—has an authentic-feeling recipe for a stovetop clambake with lobsters, shrimp, mussels, and, of course, clams. When you make it, cover your kitchen or dining room table in newspaper and have everyone throw the shells right onto the table, which is a totally juvenile delight.

CLEAN AIR Enough said.

CLIPPINGS ALBUMS In which you tape your latest snipped-out newspaper and magazine mentions. If you want to have an old-fashioned clippings album you must act quickly, while there are still newspapers and glossies from which to clip.

CLOAKS Invest in a threatening-looking hooded one; no one will dare mug you on late-night dog walks.

COBBLESTONE STREETS People complain that they're hell on cars, but they give you ample opportunity to window-peep as you're dragging along the street in your convertible, especially at night.

COFFEEHOUSE CULTURE Coffeehouses used to be an emblem of counterculture, the realm of intellectuals, the bastion of beatniks. Now they are pretty much strictly corporate enterprises, which have brought along with them a pretentious, institutional vernacular: *grande*, *venti*, and *tall*. I always order a small, medium, or large, just to be spiteful. Fight the machine, man.

COLD CREAM Which of course *must* be kept in a glass jar on your bathroom shelf; cold cream is still absolutely the best makeup remover.

fig. 6: THE COLLAPSIBLE TUBE: CONVENIENT *for* TODAY'S TRAVELER

COLD FRUIT SOUPS These were popular for centuries all over the globe but have fallen out of fashion in America in recent decades. Sweet chilled fruit soups make an erudite, refreshing first course that nicely offsets the savory second course. One of the few cold fruit soups that remains vaguely popular today is a watermelon gazpacho, but this is child's play compared to other recipes brought to America and prepared by previous generations: Russian sour cherry soup with champagne and crème fraîche; a sapphire-blue Czech blueberry with sour cream; Estonian *Leivasupp*, with black bread, cranberries, raisins, prunes, and plum brandy.

Here's a simple cold berry soup recipe unearthed from my grandmother's recipe file, which would also make a nice summer dessert:

COLD BERRY SOUP

2 cups fresh raspberries or strawberries
½ cup sugar
½ cup sour cream
2 cups ice water
½ cup red wine

Rub the berries through a fine sieve. Add sugar to taste and the sour cream. Mix. Add the water and wine and correct the sweetening. Chill.

MAKES 4 OR 5 SERVINGS.

COLOR-THEMED DINNER MENUS These amusing dinners were apparently popular toward the end of World War I in certain European circles. The 1966 *The New York Times Menu Cook Book* describes one such meal, which was "contrived to be monochromatically red": The menu consisted of a smoked salmon starter, a cold rose-tinted cherry soup, roast beef with a hot puree of beets, sliced tomato salad, a centerpiece of radishes, and raspberry sherbet topped with red ripe strawberries. The book also notes that "there is a certain humor in the fact that during a green meal in the same period Roquefort cheese appeared with the salad."

COLETTE, SIDONIE-GABRIELLE (1873–1954) This French authoress has been defiantly described as the "twentieth century's first modern woman." When she died—after publishing nearly *eighty* volumes of fiction, drama, memoir, criticism, essays, and articles—Sidonie-Gabrielle Colette was given a state funeral and mourned as a national treasure. Perhaps best known in this country for her novel *Gigi*, which was turned into a famous film and play, Colette wrote many complicated, beautiful works often focusing on strong-willed *demimondaines*, or courtesan-style mistresses.

This "erotic militant," as her biographer Judith Thurman called her, was arguably more fascinating than some of her fictional characters: Her affairs with both sexes thrilled and scandalized society; she was the first woman to report from the front lines of World War I; she had her first child at forty; and at forty-seven, she seduced her stepson.

Colette's works—even her masterpieces—are being forgotten by recent generations and are often out of print in translation. As Thurman states in an essay on the author, "It is time to rediscover them."

"COMRADE" It might not bring back the rosiest of memories for some—but considering that most of us feel like we work in some version of a Soviet-style bureaucracy, the word "comrade" is actually far more accurate than "colleague."

THE CONCORDE Once the only turbojet-powered supersonic airliner in commercial service, the Concorde flew you from New York to London in about three hours. When the plane went into service in 1976, it seemed that the future of air travel had *arrived*; you'd have thought that the next step was a jet that sped across the Atlantic at lightning speed.

Yet, in a rare instance of technological regression, the opposite happened: The Concorde was retired in 2003 (following an accident caused by debris from another plane that had used the runway five minutes earlier), and now we're back to stinky old overnight transatlantic air travel.

[PLATE 3]

Elephantine Colossus

THE CONEY ISLAND ELEPHANT Most people would likely cite the famous Cyclone roller coaster as the emblem of the iconic Brooklyn amusement park, yet in the 1880s, the "Elephantine Colossus" was the big attraction. Costing more than a quarter of a million dollars (a huge sum in those days) to construct, the elephant hotel stood 122 feet high; it contained seven floors and more than thirty rooms, and was capped by an Indian-style tented pagoda. *Scientific American* deemed the structure as important as the Washington Monument or the Statue of Liberty; it even went so far as to classify it as one of the eighth wonders of the world. Sadly, the Coney Island Elephant burned down in 1896.

Another unhappy Coney Island loss was Luna Park, whose beauty was sometimes compared to Copenhagen's famed Tivoli Gardens. Covered in many thousands of lightbulbs in a time when electricity was still a novelty, the amusement park opened to awe and fanfare in 1903; author Albert Bigelow Paine called it "an enchanted garden, of such Aladdin never dreamed." The park's bright shimmer could be seen far out to sea until it too fell victim to fire.

Coney Island once embodied joyous American amusement park and boardwalk culture, and is now about to get a likely cheesy makeover. Mercifully, three of Coney Island's rides—the Cyclone, of course, the Wonder Wheel, and the Parachute Jump—are protected as designated NYC landmarks and recognized by the National Register of Historic Places, exempting them from today's Disneyfied sensibilities.

CONSOMMÉ Up until the 1970s, these clear, strong broths were often served as a meal's first course; they are still widely consumed in France but less so here. The cold versions of this soup are extremely refreshing palate clearers in the summer. At Café Select in New York City, I was recently served a delicious clear tomato soup with bits of dill, tiny scoops of cucumber, and small tomatoes bobbing about on top; it looked like a delightful Miró collage.

TEXT CONTINUES NEXT PAGE ⟫→

Here is an old recipe for a hot consommé from *The White House Cookbook* (1887); you could practically rise from your own deathbed after eating it:

CONSOMMÉ

Take good strong stock, remove all fat from the surface, and for each quart of the stock allow the white and shell of one egg and a tablespoonful of water, well whipped together. Pour this mixture into a saucepan containing the stock; place it over the fire and heat the contents gradually, stirring often to prevent the egg from sticking to the bottom of the saucepan. Allow it to boil gently until the stock looks perfectly clear under the egg, which will rise and float upon the surface in the form of a thick white scum. Now remove it and pour it into a folded towel laid in a colander set over an earthen bowl, allowing it to run through without moving or squeezing it. Season with more salt if needed, and quickly serve very hot. This should be a clear amber color.

CONTACT SHEETS These printed outtakes of film negatives can be more evocative than the final blown-up images selected from the sheet.

"COOKING WITH GAS" Meaning "now we're really moving along," or some approximation thereof. The phrase came originally from an old advertisement for gas stoves, which declared that gas is faster, easier, cleaner, and better than cooking with wood.

"CORNY" This word has fallen out of use, yet corniness still abounds, and no word as apt has risen to take its place.

CORSETS In recent generations, the corset became an emblem of female oppression. Please put aside for a moment the modern political symbolism of the garment. A satin or silk corset with fine boning is a beautiful, functional item of clothing. Many well-made evening and wedding dresses contain corsetlike boning to help the clothes fit and hang perfectly. When it comes to wearing actual corsets, just don't pull them so damn tight: No one expects women in the twenty-first century to strive for an 18-inch waist. And anyway, women still wear ugly versions of the garments, except now they're called Spanx and control-top pantyhose. At least when you wear a satin corset, you *want* to undress in front of a man—instead of scurrying away into your bathroom and surreptitiously peeling off that ugly, synthetic, flesh-colored body stocking.

COURTING CANDLES An ingenious concept that parents of teenage children will love to revive. Used in the first half of the nineteenth century, courting candles were used to denote the amount of time a suitor could spend wooing the object of his affection. When a paramour visited the daughter of a house, the father or mother would place a candle in the room where the young couple sat. When the candle burned low, it was time for the man to leave.

The best part: A tall candle in the courtship candleholder indicated that the parents approved of your suit. But if you saw a stubby candle wedged in there, you might as well cut your losses—or elope.

COURTSHIP A practically obsolete notion. Let's bring back courtship in which love notes and letters, delivered flowers, mix tapes, and the like are involved. That would be a delightful departure from our contemporary collegiate drunken hook-up culture, and also a welcome counterpoint to the dismal recent phenomenon of "8 Minute Dating."

COVERED BRIDGES Largely built in the 1800s, many of these bridges were covered by wooden truss roofs, creating a pretty tunnel and plenty of eaves for bird nests. Most of these spans have eroded or been replaced with modern bridges and are a rare, romantic sight today.

CREAM AND SUGAR IN COFFEE Nothing looks more loveless than bitter coffee in a forlorn paper cup with skim milk and artificial sweetener. Unless, of course, that coffee is decaf on top of everything else. As with all indulgences, moderation is key.

Or not.

CRONKITE, WALTER (1916–2009) This legendary CBS anchor dominated the television news industry during one of the most volatile periods in American history. Cronkite broke the news of the Kennedy assassination and reported extensively on Vietnam, the Civil Rights movement, and Watergate; he embodied the glamour of early television journalism. His audience grew so large and his image so credible that a 1972 poll determined he was "the most trusted man in America"—surpassing even the nation's president, vice president, members of Congress, and all other journalists.

For a man of such staggering stature, Cronkite could also be a very down-to-earth guy. My father worked by his side at CBS during the late 1960s and early '70s. One day, my sister, still a toddler, visited the newsroom. At some point during the visit, she misplaced her beloved stuffed dog, Henry, and all hell broke loose. A search team was duly arranged, and after a long, exhausting manhunt, the toy was discovered sitting neatly in Cronkite's anchor chair, placed there by Cronkite himself.

CROQUET A deeply elegant way to spend an afternoon; also a deeply decadent way to spend an evening, when played indoors with empty champagne bottles as stakes.

fig. 7: NO WELL-APPOINTED
HOUSE SHOULD BE
WITHOUT ONE

Croquet used to be *wildly* popular, especially during the late 1800s, when the lack of air-conditioning meant outdoor living and amusements in the summer. It was also one of the few "sports" that both sexes could play; croquet therefore became an acceptable way for ladies to meet suitable suitors, and vice versa. A Victorian rule guide joked that "women are fond of cheating at the game, but they do so only because men like it."

CROSBY, BING (1903–1977) He makes Christmas really *feel* like Christmas.

Crosby is perhaps most closely associated with the song "White Christmas," which he sang in the film *Holiday Inn* in 1942. The nostalgic, comforting tenor of the song strongly resonated with war-weary Americans and overseas soldiers; Crosby's "White Christmas" single eventually sold more than 50 million copies, making it one of the best-selling singles in the world, according to *The Guinness Book of World Records*.

It would have a curious, eerie wartime revival three decades later. On April 30, 1975, as the North Vietnamese surrounded Saigon, the American radio station suddenly began to play Crosby's "White Christmas." Microphones were placed in front of radios, and the famous lyrics about snow and sleigh bells echoed from loudspeakers across the steamy city. The song was a code signal that the final evacuation of the remaining Americans in Saigon had begun; Crosby's usually consoling voice incited a panicked mobbing of the U.S. embassy by civilians and refugees, who swarmed helicopters waiting there to take evacuees to nearby aircraft carriers.

Playing such a definitive role in the war's end must have been grimly satisfying to Crosby, who had opposed the conflict in the first place.

CRUDITÉ PLATTERS I'll admit that this is eccentric of me, but they're just so Jackie Kennedy, circa 1961. Excepting, of course, those bloated, gummy canned olives. Those can be happily left in the crystal candy dishes of the past.

CRUMPETS Still eaten all the time in the United Kingdom, yet here in America they have practically medieval connotations. They're really just English muffins with a better name—but semantics are everything.

THE CRYSTAL PALACE This beautiful London hall was built to showcase the wonders of Britain's industrial revolution for the Great Exhibition of 1851; the shimmering facade reportedly contained more than a million feet of glass. A vast park filled with spectacular fountains (one of which spouted water 250 feet into the air) and statue-filled gardens surrounded the building, which drew millions of awestruck exhibition visitors. An emblem of Britain at the peak of its empire, the Crystal Palace rather symbolically burned down in 1936, when the empire was in decline. Yet the allure of a fantastical glass palace in the middle of a modern city remains strong.

CUCKOO CLOCKS They infuse the passing of time with humor.

CUNARD, NANCY (1896–1965) Nancy Cunard began life as a coddled British heiress to the Cunard ship fortune; her life might have been very mannered, but instead she scandalized her family and class by becoming an outspoken writer, publisher, and political activist.

Still adored by today's history-minded fashion editors and designers, Cunard grew famous in her time for her rail-thin frame and the bangles that always covered both of her arms from wrist to elbow; her contemporaries also venerated her, and she became a muse to some of the twentieth century's most distinguished writers and artists, including Wyndham Lewis, Aldous Huxley, Tristan Tzara, Ezra Pound, Louis Aragon, Ernest Hemingway, James Joyce, Constantin Brancusi, Langston Hughes, Man Ray, and William Carlos Williams.

In 1928, Cunard became romantically involved with African American jazz musician Henry Crowder; they shacked up in Harlem together, prompting outraged tabloid headlines on both sides of the Atlantic. This relationship was the first step in turning Cunard into a lifelong civil-rights activist. Her own mother's alleged reaction upon hearing the news: "Do you mean to say my daughter actually *knows* a Negro?"

Cunard subsequently published the pamphlet *Black Man and White Ladyship,* an attack on racist attitudes. She also edited *Negro: An Anthology,* collecting poetry, fiction, and nonfiction primarily by African American writers, including the now-iconic literary giants Langston Hughes, William Carlos Williams, Samuel Beckett, and Zora Neale Hurston.

She had her gentle, romantic moments as well. One of my favorite quieter anecdotes about Cunard describes her late in her life, standing on a palazzo balcony in Venice, the site of once wildly decadent *fin de siècle* and Roaring Twenties parties:

> Nancy, in a black satin gown and her signature "barbaric jewelry" and forehead bandeau, had been suddenly overcome by a vision of the past. She poured a glass of champagne into the Grand Canal—a "libation" for her former beloved: "For Henry," she said in a soft voice.

> **—Excerpted from the 2007 biography**
> ***Nancy Cunard: Heiress, Muse, Political Idealist* by Lois Gordon**

CURLS ON LITTLE GIRLS Little girls *always* used to get Shirley Temple–style curls put into their hair for fancy occasions. Before the advent of hot rollers and curling irons, women used bobby pins and rags to curl their daughters' hair (and their own); one sees early-twentieth-century references to "spit" curls and "rag" curls (sometimes known as "Depression curls," since they were an inexpensive way to maintain an expensive-looking head during that impoverished era).

My mother-in-law has poignant memories about how her 1950s little-girl curls were created: Every Saturday night, her hair would be washed with Halo shampoo; afterward, she'd get a pink Helene Curtis crème rinse. Her hair would be set in curlers, with a little bit of Dippity-do "setting gel" applied to the hair ends; then, her head swathed in one of those vinyl bonnet hair dryers, she would patiently wait for the curls to materialize, usually while watching television.

TEXT CONTINUES NEXT PAGE ⟫→

HOW TO MAKE PIN CURLS:

1. Section off a small amount of hair.

2. Comb it and wind it around your finger; make sure that it's flat, not twisted.

3. When the entire strand is wound, slide your finger out and press it against your scalp; then secure it with a bobby pin across the center of the curl and slide another bobby pin over the curl, perpendicular to the first pin.

4. Continue making these curls over your whole head, making sure that they're all wound in the same direction.

5. The curls *must* be dried completely; you can leave the pin curls in overnight while you sleep (covering them with a kerchief or silk scarf), or dry them amply with a hair dryer set on the lowest setting (you can see why those now-obsolete bonnet dryers used to be so popular; that way, you could varnish your nails while modern technology dried your curls for you).

6. Gently take out the pins and comb lightly.

CURSES AND HEXES You can wield some ultraspecific ones. A highly satisfying way to settle scores.

CUTTING GARDENS An integral part of the rural Victorian household: an informal flower patch, often planted near the kitchen garden, where flowers were allowed to grow wild. This garden was used for cuttings that could then be used in indoor arrangements.

My cutting garden would be absolutely brimming with lavender.

DACHÉ, LILLY (C. 1893–1989) French-born Lilly Daché was the most celebrated milliner in the United States during the 1930s and '40s—a time when hats were the centerpieces of a woman's wardrobe; as the *New York Times* noted in Daché's obituary, during the Depression, "women with limited funds tended to buy new hats instead of new clothes. In the 1940s clothing fabric was in restricted supply because of World War II, and hats continued in demand because they were showy."

Daché's wildly creative hat designs were coveted by all fashion-minded females and touted as status *objets* by practically every major movie star of the day, including Greta Garbo, Marlene Dietrich, Carmen Miranda, and Jean Harlow. Like so many fashion industry powerhouse doyennes of her era, Daché was a rags-to-riches icon: Arriving in America in 1924 with thirteen dollars in her pocket (or so the story goes), she saw a sign in a window on a shop on Broadway saying "Milliner Wanted," and history was set in motion. She eventually bought the shop from the owner and soon became a household name.

Daché could be as flamboyant as some of her designs; according to one of her biographers, Daché often conducted business from her bed, "dictating letters, buying supplies, designing, and interviewing employees while wrapped in a leopard-skin rug." Sometimes meetings were held in her bathroom, where Daché would give orders from a deep bubble bath. Brunette celebrities were guided to a fitting room decorated in shimmering silver; blonde clients were ushered into a dressing room of gleaming gold. Bells adorned Daché's leopard-skin slippers, perhaps "to warn her girls of her approach, a job later undertaken by her armful of jingling bangles."

Such ladies usually are the best perpetuators of their own self-crafted legends; so let's finish up with one of Daché's more famous exclamations:

> "I like beautiful shoes in gay colors, with thick platforms and high heels. I like splashy jewelry that clinks when I walk, and I like my earrings big. I am Lilly Daché, milliner de luxe."

DAGUERREOTYPES Popular in the nineteenth century, these metal-set, vaguely three-dimensional photographs have a slightly enchanted look about them, as though part of the souls of their long-dead subjects are still alive inside them. It's tempting to bring back such means of immortality, however minor.

DAISIES Like many modern cocktails and restaurant entrées, modern flower arrangements can be overwrought with ingredients. Sometimes it's so lovely to get an innocent, cheerful bouquet of daisies.

DANCING People got to foxtrot, tango, and Charleston in the 1920s; they jitterbugged in the '30s; went swing dancing in the '50s; and did the Twist in the '60s. There was disco in the '70s; in the '80s, everyone groped the hell out of each other while "Dirty Dancing"; and the early '90s brought about "Vogueing," which looked sort of dumb but was better than nothing, I guess. What dance does the current generation have?

Incidentally, waltzing was considered terribly scandalous when it first came onto the European scene in the eighteenth century: It was the first dance in which the couple danced in a "closed position," with the man's hand around the waist of the woman. Up until this time, court dances were stately and solemn procession-style dances, performed in separate positions. In 1816, England's Prince Regent included the waltz in a London ball; a few days after the ball, the following blustery editorial appeared in *The Times of London*:

> We remarked with pain that the indecent foreign dance called the Waltz was introduced (we believe for the first time) at the English court on Friday last . . . National morals depend on national habits: and it is quite sufficient to cast one's eyes on the voluptuous intertwining of the limbs and close compressure on the bodies, in their dance, to conclude that it is indeed far removed from the modest reserve which has hitherto been considered dis-tinctive of English females. So long as this obscene display was confined to prostitutes and adulteresses, we did not think it deserving of notice; but now [that] it is attempted to be forced on the respectable classes of society by the evil examples of their superiors, we feel it a duty to warn every parent against exposing his daughter to so fatal a contagion.

"DAPPER" Taken in their totality, the various meanings of this old-fashioned word conjure up a very specific creature:

> **dap·per** \'dap-ər\ *adj* **1** : neat; trim; smart **2** : lively and brisk **3** : small and active

One imagines a neat, trim, small man, taking brisk little steps up the street, dusting off his lapel and straightening his tie as he goes; he wears a hat, of course. Such a man would always turn up to a date with a bouquet of flowers and give a little bow at the door. No wonder the word went out of fashion: These days, there are too few men to whom it applies.

DAVIS, BETTE (1908–1989) She used to *own* Hollywood, and these days, all people can remember about her is the vague phrase "Bette Davis eyes"—the title of a grating song written in the 1980s that wasn't even *about* Bette Davis.

Many actresses of her era founded their legends on their perfect bone structures and lavish wardrobes; yet Davis, who was neither classically beautiful nor a clotheshorse, succeeded by vigorously devoting herself to her craft. She was willing to play daring, unsympathetic roles—like Baby Jane Hudson in the hair-raising *What Ever Happened to Baby Jane?*—and was a forerunner to Meryl Streep in terms of versatility.

Bette Davis: strong-minded, strong-willed, self-deprecating, and sharp as a knife. On my death day, I want to be propped up in bed, watching *The Man Who Came to Dinner, Jezebel*, and *All About Eve*.

DE ACOSTA, MERCEDES (1893–1968) Silver-screen legends Greta Garbo and Marlene Dietrich hated each other; in fact, Dietrich was imported from Germany by Paramount Pictures specifically to compete with Garbo, then under contract to MGM. Regardless of this arrangement, they likely would have hated one another anyway: Garbo was one of the world's great introverts, while Dietrich's gusto for the limelight and extroversion has been rivaled only by Madonna's. The women rarely spoke but silently battled each other—especially over an opportunistic woman named Mercedes de Acosta, who was an intimate companion to both at one point.

A well-born socialite, poet, and writer, de Acosta supposedly ravished nearly every female star in Old Hollywood, including Alla Nazimova, Eva Le Gallienne, Isadora Duncan, Katharine Cornell, Ona Munson, Adele Astaire, and Tallulah Bankhead. But her *coup d'etat* was the Garbo-Dietrich tug-of-war, which gave her international notoriety and standing. Yet all good things come to an end: de Acosta found herself cast as a social leper after publishing her autobiography, *Here Lies the Heart*, in 1960, which gave intimate details about those with whom she'd been intimate. Garbo cut her off entirely, snubbing her on the street and even refusing to visit de Acosta on her deathbed.

While de Acosta herself sounds a bit too predatory for my taste (Dietrich's daughter referred to her as "Dracula"), *Here Lies the Heart* still makes for a fascinating read, but it's out of print, rare, and expensive. The next best thing: a book called *The Girls: Sappho Goes to Hollywood* by Diana McLellan, which outlines the infamous love triangle in gossipy detail.

DE WOLFE, ELSIE (C. 1865–1950) Sixty years after her death, she remains one of America's most influential decorators. Elsie de Wolfe almost single-handedly ushered out the dark, cramped-room aesthetic of Victorian interiors; in its place she arranged delicate eighteenth-century French-inspired furniture, clean surfaces, and open entertaining areas. "I opened the doors and windows of America and let the air and sunshine in," she once said.

Her ingenuity went far beyond color-coordinating fabrics; according to biographers Annette Tapert and Diana Edkins in *The Power of Style*, de Wolfe pioneered the wall light switch, invented the bed rest with arms and an armchair that transforms into a chaise longue, introduced drawers to vanity tables, and laid down the first parquet floors. She popularized chintz and pillows embroidered with sayings, and even introduced the concept of the cocktail party; at her own such fetes, she served "Pink Lady" cocktails ($1/3$ gin, $1/3$ grapefruit juice, $1/3$ Cointreau).

While many of de Wolfe's clients were rich beyond belief, she also predated Martha Stewart's do-it-yourself empire by decades. Through columns in the *Ladies' Home Journal* and her own book, *The House in Good Taste* (1914), she advised women on how to decorate and entertain: "Plates should be hot, hot, hot; glasses cold, cold, cold; and table decorations low, low, low." Her best and simplest more-dash-than-cash advice: Use plenty of mirrors to maximize the sense of space in a room, along with "plenty of optimism and white paint."

DEAN, JAMES (1931–1955) The symbol of youthful rebellion, this actor ushered in an era of teenage insurrection against bourgeois 1950s values. Conversely, so many of today's youthful icons have all the attributes of materialistic, fully socialized adults. Nothing depresses me more than those Chanel purse–laden trollops on *Gossip Girl*, who avidly anticipate lives centered around charity ball committees and Botox.

If these represent the values and aspirations of the up-and-coming generation, then maybe the old saying is true: "Youth is wasted on the young."

DEATH

I think we should bring death back into our lives. Socrates taught that we should "practice death" daily to help us remember what's really important. And the ancient Romans used to carve "MM" on the bases of statues and the trunks of trees. The letters stand for *Memento Mori*—"Remember Death." This wasn't a sign of morbidity, but a way to bring perspective into our lives and a mental tool with which to overcome our fear of the unknown and come to terms with life's only inevitability. Bringing back death can help us appreciate life to the fullest.

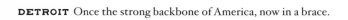

—Arianna Huffington • FOUNDER AND EDITOR IN CHIEF, *THE HUFFINGTON POST*

DETROIT Once the strong backbone of America, now in a brace.

fig. 8: ASHES TO ASHES

DIARIES As one of Oscar Wilde's characters said in *The Importance of Being Earnest*: "I never travel without my diary. One should always have something sensational to read in the train."

As usual, Wilde cuts to the heart of the matter: Diaries are meant to be deeply secretive—and casually available to scandalize those around you. Old-fashioned diaries came adorned with a lock and key; if you choose this variety, make sure that the lock is weak and pickable with a nail file, and leave the book lying around the house whenever you go out.

THE DINGO BAR Opened in 1923, the Dingo Bar resided at 10 rue Delambre in Paris's Montparnasse; *le dingo* was slang for "the crazy man." One of the few drinking establishments that was open all night, it became a Lost Generation haunt. This is where Hemingway first met Fitzgerald and where Nancy Cunard held court with all her famous clacking bracelets; Man Ray and Isadora Duncan would waft over from their respective apartments right across the street.

Eventually the Dingo lost its luster and went out of business, depriving us of what would have been a grand Lost Generation pilgrimage site. Now the premises are home to a restaurant called the Auberge de Venise.

DISCREET VOICES A major blight of our era is the public cell-phone voice. There is something about holding a phone in one's hand in a restaurant, train, or store that compels people to absolutely bellow out the most intimate or mundane details of their lives for all to hear. Here's a news flash: Cell phones have sensitive microphones; if you *whisper,* the person on the other end can hear you.

DISCUSSION SOCIETIES Real discussion is a dying art. Let's revive those evening discussion societies like the ones attended by the Schlegel sisters in *Howards End*, where they talked about art, philanthropy, politics, and other self-improving subjects. Chat rooms, status updates, twittering, and message boards are a poor substitute for interaction in real rooms with three-dimensional people. Anonymous Internet postings try to pass for discussion societies but are not the same thing; too often they breed animosity instead of constructive discourse.

DIVINITY Most popular in the early twentieth century, this white or pastel-colored meringue-like confection is still consumed in the South but less so elsewhere. It was named "divinity" because it tasted divine—and still does, when you can find it. Here's a simple 1914 recipe from the *Second Edition of the Neighborhood Cookbook* by Portland's Council of Jewish Women:

DIVINITY

3 cups sugar
1 cup Karo corn syrup
¾ cup water

3 well-beaten whites of eggs
2 cups chopped walnuts
1 tablespoon vanilla

Boil first three ingredients until quite brittle, then pour slowly and gradually into the eggs and beat until it stiffens. Add vanilla and nuts and pour onto a buttered platter. When cold, cut in squares.

DOGHOUSES Our dogs would never go near them, but they looked great in the backyard regardless: very *Tom and Jerry* chic.

"DOLLAR PRINCESSES" Along with "dollar duchesses," this Gilded Age term describing the American heiresses to newly made industrial fortunes, who were exported (often by socially ambitious parents) to Europe to trade dollars for titles. Increasingly impoverished European aristocrats courted the hell out of them in a bid to shore up their dwindling resources and crumbling estates. According to *Time* magazine, "between 1874 and 1910, more than 160 U.S. heiresses staged the first lend-lease program. They bestowed more than $160 million on the stately homes of England and the Continent."

SOME OF THE MOST PROMINENT DOLLAR PRINCESSES:

••• **CARA ROGERS.** Her family fortune derived from prescient investments in American petroleum, copper, steel, mining, and railways; she eventually became Lady Fairhaven

••• **CONSUELO YZNAGA.** A wealthy Southern belle who became the Duchess of Manchester

• • • **JENNIE JEROME.** Born in Brooklyn to a financier and speculator father, she later became Lady Randolph Churchill and mother of the great Winston Churchill

• • • **MARY LEITER.** The dry goods and real estate heiress who became Lady Curzon, Vicereine of India

The most famous D.P., however, was Consuelo Vanderbilt (an heiress to the stupendous Vanderbilt railroad fortune), whose 1895 marriage to the Duke of Marlborough caused an international press fever. How the deal was sealed: The Duke was reportedly enticed to the altar by a dowry offer of $2.5 million (more than $60 million in today's money) in railroad stock, plus money to make repairs to his Blenheim Palace. The new Duchess of Marlborough produced two sons ("an heir and a spare," she quipped) before calling it quits on the ultimately unhappy marriage.

We're hardly drowning in such dollar princesses these days, given that our economy has been in the dumps. Still, it's an amusing term that speaks volumes, should the need for it ever arise again.

DOMINO MAGAZINE Its demise was so recent; the grief is still raw.

DOOR-TO-DOOR PEDDLERS Especially knife sharpeners. My knives and scissors are always dull.

DOOR-HOLDING ETIQUETTE It's not a question of outmoded chivalry; it's a question of politeness. Some people seem to have forgotten even the most rudimentary manners when it comes to door etiquette: like letting someone who is outside in the rain or snow enter before shoving imperiously past him or her. Also popular these days: letting a front door slam shut on a person carrying heaps of packages or pushing a baby carriage.

DOROTHY DRAPER–DESIGNED AIRPLANE CABINS A very famous decorator in America from the 1930s to the '60s, Dorothy Draper is now being knocked off left and right: Her boldly striped walls and rococo flourishes are everywhere these days. I wish that someone in the airline industry would start knocking her off as well; most airplane cabins today

TEXT CONTINUES NEXT PAGE ⟩⟩⟩→

[PLATE 4]

Honor or Death

resemble dowdy dentist waiting rooms; those ratty, pilly airplane blankets often look like they've been used in a children's camp cabin for approximately three decades.

In the late '50s, General Dynamics hired Draper to decorate the interior of its next-generation jet, the Convair 880. The result—which included walls stenciled with gold planets and stars, Mondrian-inspired lounge walls, gold Mylar-covered seat bases and panels, and gold seat buckles—was beautiful enough to use as a fashion-spread backdrop in a 1958 edition of *Harper's Bazaar.* The magazine proclaimed: "Mrs. Draper has scrapped the merely utilitarian look for bold, fresh color; has eliminated the locked-up-in-a-closet feeling with an illusion of air and space. Seats are not only comfortable, they're brilliantly striped."

"DOUGH" Using this word in lieu of "money" will garner you lots of retro street cred. Equally pleasing synonyms include "bread" and "clams."

DOUBLE FEATURES Perfect for long, rainy November afternoons, and for prolonging first-date make-out sessions. Let's also bring back prefeature cartoon shorts.

DRAWBRIDGES AND MOATS For the privacy-minded homeowner: These features are *much* more creative than the been-there-done-that two-story hedge.

DRESSING FOR YOUR SHAPE Too few women today know to take this notion seriously, with often-disastrous consequences. As famed costume designer and stylist Edith Head once said, "Fit the dress to the girl, not the girl to the dress." It's a rule to live by.

DRESSING GOWNS Designer Christian Dior once admonished, "Our mothers used to take great care about dressing-gowns and they were quite right: . . . too many women [today] neglect it." To him, it was just as important "to look always right especially in the intimacy of your home" as it was for an evening on the town. Take his advice: Buy an elegant dressing gown; wear it on weekend mornings, leaving the faded Juicy Couture tracksuit in the back of the hamper.

DRESSING SCREENS A good perch on which to display your latest clothing purchase or to air an evening gown you'll be wearing later that evening.

DRESSING UP *For casinos*: Lady luck is attracted to those who look the part.

For dinner: People used to do it every night: dinner jackets and evening gowns. Now showing up to dinner can be like getting slopped at a trough, and people often dress accordingly.

For flying: These days, airport attire is an assault on beauty—and often decency. Flying used to be considered a glamorous event, as did arriving; people wore their Sunday best for the occasion.

DRIVING GLOVES They make you feel like you're heading to the Riviera, even if you're just driving to the supermarket.

"DROOL TIME"

I say this as one who fully appreciates the break I catch by having a tool for avoiding myself as good as a smartphone; therefore I fully realize what size gift horse I am looking in the mouth. But the memories nag, calling forth the frequent and intense pleasures of my everyday life before mobile phones. I remember riding the bus home from work, a forty-five-minute trip, and having fantasy wash away anxiety. No matter what happened during the day, I was able to count on the healing power of those daydreams on the ride home, each one teased out of hiding by the most optimistic, personal, and individual part of me. The option was to read something, which made me carsick, or put my head against the window and watch my thoughts graze free for the better part of an hour with absolutely no competition for my attention, even if I wished for some. I used to call it "drool time." I miss it.

—James L. Brooks • PRODUCER; DIRECTOR; SCREENWRITER; EXECUTIVE PRODUCER, *THE SIMPSONS*

DUELS Because litigation is so cost-prohibitive, and takes too long as well.

DUMBWAITERS Truly the stuff of creaking whimsy; wonderful places to hide from overly inquisitive relatives; equally cunning perches from which to spy on various unsuspecting members of the household: much chicer than a "nanny cam."

DUNCE CAPS Not for children, which is cruel, but rather for the legions of irritating and incompetent adults one meets each day. Like that "genius" at the Apple Store's so-called Genius Bar, who spilled a coffee into my laptop last summer. Perhaps someone should invent a tissue box of disposable paper ones, for easy distribution.

See also CHARM SCHOOL

"DUNGAREES" The word returns denim to its charmingly humble origins.

DUTCH DOORS Also called "half-doors," these old-school doors are divided horizontally so that you can open the top half while keeping the bottom one shut. In the old days, the Dutch door kept small children and household pets inside (and unwanted varmints out), while letting in light and nice breezes, and allowing the mistress of the household to conduct business with various vendors and neighbors. I also love screen door culture; both door models are underused in today's perpetually air-conditioned homes.

E

EAR HORNS The buzz from hearing aids must get awfully tiresome.

EATING WHAT YOU ARE SERVED

In my White House days, I became accustomed to receiving a telephone call from the office of a most important senator on the afternoons of state dinners, asking what was on that night's menu. Based on how the senator felt about the food he would be served, the staff member would either say, "Thank you very much," and hang up, because everything was okay, or would issue a breathless "I'm so sorry, but he will be unable to attend tonight because of a suddenly-called important meeting." *The important meeting* was, of course, the fact that the senator disliked duck, which was on that night's menu. He preferred to eat steak that evening with his colleagues in the Senate dining room, so that was what he did!

We should remember, of course, that back "in the old days," guests could not demand that certain foods be served to them or not be served to them. As my mother would say, "Eat what's put in front of you; that's all the discussion there will be!"

— *Letitia Baldrige* • ETIQUETTE EXPERT; JACQUELINE KENNEDY'S
WHITE HOUSE SOCIAL SECRETARY

ECCENTRICITY True eccentricity—the sort that was once worshipped among certain outlandish upper-class provocateurs—is said to have gone out of style after World War I; people apparently did not have the where-withal for it anymore. A page from *Infinite Variety*, a biography about the Marchesa Luisa Casati—whose peculiar parties, spectacular fortune, zoo of exotic pets, cosmetically induced deathlike pallor, and dabblings with the occult made her the poster girl of elite eccentricity—describes her postwar fall from grace:

> Casati's style, regardless of its timeless outrageousness, was now consid-
> ered dated. Even her close friend Baron de Meyer commented in the bon
> ton bible, *Harper's Bazaar:* "Taste and exquisite reticence have become
> one of the fine arts. Eccentricity is thought a crime and is actually the most
> démodé and unfashionable thing a woman can indulge in nowadays!"

Indeed, eccentricity often goes sour once the novelty of its practitioner has waned—yet it is good for us to have eccentric figures around, to serve as a reminder that life doesn't have to be lived so linearly—or taken so literally.

EGGBEATERS They look like good exercise.

fig. 9: BUILD MUSCLE
TONE

ELBOW GLOVES For evening *and* daytime. Elbow gloves in bold colors have recently been featured again in elite magazine editorials; they look gorgeous and women look gorgeous in them, but such gloves haven't exactly made a hit in the mass market, for whatever reason. You can lead a horse to water, but you can't make it drink.

fig. 10: DELECTABLY FUN TO REMOVE

ELEGANCE

"Elegance [is] rarely found today. Women are not brought up to know about it and therefore lack even the desire to acquire it."

—Marlene Dietrich

Elegantly stated.

ELEVATOR OPERATORS One sees too few men in hats and smart uniforms these days.

"ELEVENSES" Simply a late-morning snack, sort of like teatime in the morning. I'm all for taking as many luxuriant breaks as possible throughout the day.

ELIZABETH ARDEN'S GYMNASIUM MODERNE

In 1936, beauty tycoon Elizabeth Arden opened her celebrated Gymnasium Moderne, a state-of-the-art gymnastics and dance department that stretched over an entire floor of her Fifth Avenue flagship store. Clients were encouraged to "unfurl like a flower"—inspired by artist Georgia O'Keeffe's specially commissioned painting *Miracle Flower*, which dominated the wall space. They took yoga classes on satin-backed cashmere yoga mats— taking them home at $65 a pop—and boosted blood circulation with a session on the fabled Arden "tilt boards" before choosing from a light lunch menu devised by "Nutritionist to the Stars" Gayelord Hauser (who kept Greta Garbo and the Duchess of Windsor thin). Eurythmics classes were held on arguably the best-sprung dance floor in town, and, as an added bonus, clients could sign up for fencing sessions with Olympic gold medalist and world champion Italian swordsman Aldo Nadi, who conducted his classes dressed in black velvet leggings and a custom-tailored white jacket.

Not to be outdone, Arden's archrival, cosmetics mogul Helena Rubinstein, countered by opening her own architecturally and artistically acclaimed salon at 715 Fifth Avenue, filled with murals by Pallavicini, sculptures by Malvina Hoffman, and rugs by Joan Miró. But only Miss Arden had the great Nadi. *En garde!*

—*Lindy Woodhead* • AUTHOR, *WAR PAINT: MADAME HELENA RUBINSTEIN AND MISS ELIZABETH ARDEN, THEIR LIVES, THEIR TIMES, THEIR RIVALRY*

ELOCUTION Not to be confused with "electrocution," elocution is the study of artful speaking. Today's general manner of speaking is so rapid and undecipherable that half the time you never know if the speaker is coming or going.

ELOPING Marriage as an act of defiance, instead of an act of conformity.

ENCYCLOPEDIA SETS We need these stodgy old stalwarts, now that we dwell in the Wikipedia world of ever-alterable facts.

ENGLISH NANNIES In the adored children's series *Eloise*, which features a precocious six-year-old girl growing up in New York City's Plaza Hotel, the title character's English nanny is always impeccably dressed with a dickey-fronted blouse, corset ("which is enormously large but which is very good for her back"), and eight hairpins made out of bones. She never makes Eloise clean her room, dons a kimono in the morning, loves room service, and drinks Pilsner beer and smokes Players while watching boxing in the drawing room. In short: the ideal childhood companion.

ENTERTAINING AT HOME Meeting friends at restaurants or bars can become a repetitive, expensive bore. However, a dinner party invitation at someone's house is always an honor—not to mention that it feels far more exclusive.

There are endless occasions to celebrate with at-home parties: May Day, half-birthdays, Summer or Winter Solstice, Patriot's Day, Tax Day (this is clearly a gallows-humor fête), and so on.

EPITAPHS Preferably humorous ones. Writer Dorothy Parker was once asked to compose her epitaph; her offering: "Excuse My Dust" (this phrase actually does adorn her memorial site in Baltimore). She also came up with another one: "This Is on Me." My favorite epitaph hails from British comedy series *Absolutely Fabulous*; in one episode, someone suggests that the debauched main character, Edwina Monsoon, should someday lie under a stone that declares: "EDDY: STILL NO THINNER."

[PLATE 5]

Excellent for inconspicuous eavesdropping

ERMINE Once the fur donned by royals—but cuter as pets than as trim on a cape.

ESPALIERED FRUIT TREES An increasingly obsolete gardening art that spans back to ancient Roman times. Espaliered fruit trees are trained to grow flat against a wall or fence, their branches fanned out to resemble peacock tails; they can also be trimmed into a traditional triangular tree shape. Either way, they are an astonishing sight for modern eyes.

It's a little bit odd that these creations are now out of fashion, considering how space-efficient they are: You'd think they'd be a perfect match for today's pygmy urban gardens.

ESTATES As in tapestry-filled castles that preside over countless acres of land; the sort that boast stocked fish ponds and pheasants trailing over vast lawns, a motley array of nosy, uniformed staffers, and a wing where the most eccentric relative languishes away, remembering her glory years as a promising debutante.

EVENING NEWS SIGN-OFF LINES Two of CBS News's greatest anchors had famed signature sign-off lines, with which they would end each evening news broadcast. Seen as a consoling ritual in often-tumultuous times, viewers could be assured that Edward Murrow would unfailingly wish them "Good night, and good luck," and that Walter Cronkite would inform them matter-of-factly: "And that's the way it is."

EVENING STROLLS A civilized after-dinner occupation, as opposed to throwing yourself down onto a sofa and watching reruns of *America's Next Top Model* or *Bridezillas*.

EVENING WATCHES Today people tend to only own one watch and wear it at all times, but most watches look inelegant when worn with evening wear. Victorians owned evening watches to wear to the theater, dinners, and other grand occasions: Jewels often adorned the watch faces, and the straps were made of satin cord or ribbon. Still popular in the 1920s and '30s, evening watches were updated with Art Deco designs and glittered on the arms of ladies making the rounds at speakeasies and supper clubs.

EXOTIC PETS I don't mean iguanas, snakes, or potbellied pigs, whose exoticness has become almost commonplace. I'm thinking more along the lines of *cheetahs*. Eccentric Italian heiress Luisa Casati famously used to stalk the streets of Venice at midnight wearing nothing beneath her furs, accompanied by her pet cheetahs on diamond-studded leashes; other Casati pets included albino blackbirds, white peacocks, ocelots, and boa constrictors (one of which regrettably escaped during a Casati visit to the Paris Ritz).

Another cheetah owner was the great Josephine Baker, famed for dancing in 1920s Paris clad only in a hula skirt of bananas. In her memoir, *D.V.*, *Vogue*'s Diana Vreeland claims that Baker took her cheetah to her local Parisian movie theater; afterward, the mistress and pet would run down the theater's stairs and leap into a white-and-silver Rolls Royce waiting outside. Who wouldn't risk an occasional mauling for *that* degree of glamour?

Poet Lord Byron had a famous pet during his student years at Cambridge University; enraged by college bylaws forbidding him from keeping a dog in his rooms, he went out and purchased a former dancing bear, arguing that the university rule book did not specifically bar the keeping of bears. According to campus legend, Lord Byron was often seen bathing the animal in Trinity College's famed Great Court fountain.

Actress Tallulah Bankhead owned a pet lion named Winston; it's difficult to say who had the sharper bite.

On a quieter note, I've also always been enchanted by Karen Blixen's little white owl in the film *Out of Africa*, the one that sits sweetly on her vanity table—although I wouldn't have the stomach to keep owl food (i.e., bugs and mice) in the freezer along with the popsicles.

EXTERNAL KITCHENS Kitchens often used to occupy an outhouse building to avoid burning down the main house if a grease fire broke out. I vote that we bring back this arrangement; that way, no one will know when you've burned the garlic (again) or had another such cooking debacle.

F

FABERGÉ EGGS They really are the perfect gift for the person who has everything. To illustrate: Every year, Russian Czar Alexander III gave one to his wife, Czarina Maria Feodorovna. The first Imperial Fabergé Easter Egg appeared to be a common egg; covered in white enamel, it opened up to reveal a gilt-lined interior. A separate hollow golden yolk inside contained another surprise: a golden hen with eyes of ruby. And *then*, inside the hen was nestled a diamond-set replica of the Imperial crown and a tiny ruby egg.

The Imperial Fabergé eggs grew more extravagant each year. My favorite: a 1900 cobalt-blue egg encrusted with 1,618 rose-cut diamonds, which contained a wind-up elephant. Arguably the most famous: the Coronation Egg of 1897, a gold, enamel, diamond, and ruby confection that contained a bejeweled replica of the Imperial coach (complete with moving wheels, opening doors, actual C-spring shocks, and a tiny folding step-stair) that had carried Czarina Alexandra to the actual coronation a year earlier.

Many of the jeweled eggs made by the House of Fabergé before the Russian Revolution have been lost, and perhaps destroyed. The Coronation Egg survives: In 2004, it was sold by Sotheby's as part of a Fabergé collection in a private sale to Russian mining and oil billionaire Viktor Vekselberg. While the egg's actual purchase price has never been disclosed, Sotheby's estimated its worth to be around $24 million before the sale.

FAINTING COUCHES Lately some retailers have been marketing settees under the false label "fainting couches." A real fainting couch tilts downward on one side like a slide; in the days when ladies grew lightheaded from their too-tight corsets, their servants would toss them onto a fainting couch with their heads pointing toward the floor—that way the blood would rush to their heads and revive them.

These quaint furnishings still have practical applications today. As Charlotte of *Charlotte's Web* fame said, "When I'm hanging head-down at the top of my web, that's when I do my thinking, because then all of the blood is in my head."

Perhaps every office should have one to boost employee creativity.

FAKE VOMIT And other gag items of that tenor: fake dog poop, squirting lapel flowers and cameras, whoopee cushions, disappearing ink, fake blood capsules, fake parking tickets, and my childhood favorite: those fake arrow-through-the-head headbands.

FALSE EYELASHES Women in the 1960s sometimes wore little ones ("minis") just in the corners of their eyes to "open them up," according to one former fan. They supposedly make all the difference in the world, especially when you're hungover and your eyes look like puffy little slits.

FAMILY BIBLES Families used to record the dates of weddings, deaths, births, and other landmark occasions on the inside of the house Bible's front cover. The Bible would become an heirloom, documenting generations of the family's personal history. It would be nice to revive some version of this tradition, and Bibles are actually almost beside the point: A much-beloved cookbook would also do the trick nicely. That way you could hand down culinary and social history at the same time.

FAMILY CRESTS Historically, family crests adorned flags, signet rings, and household stationery; they were also sometimes engraved on the backs of family silverware, which, according to old customs, was placed facedown on the table so that the crests were on display.

Go online and see if you can find a crest that matches your family name; but making up your own might be more fun. Put whatever you like on it, from lions and dragons to the family Labrador.

FAMILY "HOUSES" As in, "House of Astor." Referring to your clan in this manner instantly polishes up the most meager or dubious of lineages.

FANCY-DRESS WEDDINGS Masked-ball weddings enjoyed a brief vogue in the early twentieth century; why not bring back this custom and give guests a *fun* participatory event to look forward to? So many weddings today resemble formulaic, business-casual affairs.

FANS, ELECTRIC While divine on humid August days, air-conditioning is severing us further from the natural world. Our windows and doors are closed to the sounds of summer: rain, crickets, thunder, wind. When I was little, central air wasn't yet ubiquitous; I had a fan in my bedroom, which made the cloth on the canopy bed flutter. I could hear the nighttime sounds in the yard and the creaking of the old house. Yes, it was hot, but that made my dreams more poignant.

When we eventually got air-conditioning, it meant sore throats and boring dreams.

FANS, HANDHELD In countless cultures over the centuries, handheld fans used to be a crucial part of a lady's' wardrobe; in Georgian times, both men and women carried them, and they were hideously expensive. Wielders of these fans could speak without using words. A 1797 English publication, *Fanology or Ladies' Conversation Fan*, contained a list of gestures and their symbolism:

- • • Placing your fan near your heart = *I love you.*
- • • A closed fan resting on the right eye = *When can I see you?*
- • • A half-closed fan pressed to the lips = *You may kiss me.*
- • • Touching the tip of the fan with a finger = *I wish to speak to you.*
- • • Letting the fan rest on the right cheek = *Yes.*
- • • Letting the fan rest on the left cheek = *No.*
- • • Dropping the fan = *We will be friends.*
- • • Fanning slowly = *I am married.*
- • • Fanning quickly = *I am engaged.*
- • • Carrying an open fan in the left hand = *Come and talk to me.*
- • • Twirling the fan in the right hand = *I love another.*
- • • Twirling the fan in the left hand = *We are being watched.*
- • • Shutting a fully open fan slowly = *I promise to marry you.*
- • • Drawing the fan across the eyes = *I am sorry.*
- • • Opening a fan wide = *Wait for me.*

fig. 11: A REFINED LANGUAGE *of* NUANCE

FASHION ILLUSTRATION People often talk about life imitating art and vice versa; fashion illustration used to make you want to *live* your life as the high art depicted in magazines. It went on the decline in the 1930s, when photography bumped drawings and paintings from the pages of glossies and newspapers. As one contemporary fashion editor recently wrote, "Illustration lives on, but in the position of a poor relative."

While photography is deeply unlikely to yield its throne back to illustration anytime soon, not everyone agrees that photos always showcase clothes to their best advantage. As designer Yves Saint Laurent lamented in the foreword to a book on the great illustrator Kenneth Paul Block:

> However much I admire photographers, I have to admit their work is done to the detriment of the design. It is often the background that takes pride of place. In the case of an illustration, it is the opposite. The design is well and truly present and alive. . . . [fashion illustrators] were for so long the painstaking partners of couturiers.

Masters such as the aforementioned Mr. Block, René Bouché, Cecil Beaton, and Andy Warhol used to make clothing look *incredibly* glamorous—far more so than today's fashion magazine editorials featuring couture-clad models striking robot poses against a gray backdrop month after month.

FAT FROG A violently green, frog-shaped Good Humor ice cream pop from the 1980s. For the *life* of me, I can't figure out why they disappeared from our supermarket freezers, unless they were secretly proven to cause birth defects or something. The ice cream truck in my neighborhood was always running out of them; there was once a fistfight over the last one.

Fat Frog connoisseurs will remember with equal fondness "Bubble O' Bill" pops—an ice cream cowboy head on a stick with a bubblegum-ball nose and a "hole" in the hat, designed to represent a gunshot. These days, BO'B is only available in Australia, making a twenty-four-hour plane ride to Sydney seem worth it.

FAT RASCALS The White House menus of America's first ladies have long influenced the way the rest of America eats. "Fat Rascals" were breakfast biscuits, and a tremendously popular treat from First Lady Edith Roosevelt's personal cookbook, (which allegedly still resides on a kitchen shelf in the Roosevelts' Sagamore Hill home in Oyster Bay, New York). It was apparently one of President Teddy Roosevelt's favorite recipes—and the possible culprit behind that round hill of a stomach.

FAT RASCALS

4 cups of flour
1 teaspoon of salt
¼ cup of sugar
4 teaspoons of baking powder

1½ cups of butter
1 pound of dried currants
1 cup of milk

Sift the flour with the salt, sugar, and baking powder. Mix well. Cut in the butter. Then stir in the dried currants. Mix well again and add the milk, little by little. With each addition, mix with a fork until a soft dough forms. Roll the dough approximately ½ inch thick on a lightly floured board. Use a 2-inch-round cutter to shape the biscuits. Bake biscuits on an ungreased cookie sheet until nicely browned. Bake in a hot (450 degrees F) oven about 12 minutes. When done, remove from oven, split and butter each biscuit, and serve piping hot. Makes approximately two dozen.

Served with ham and gooseberry jam, they make a perfectly lovely Sunday morning breakfast.

Food and appetite played an important role in the Roosevelts' lives: "Simple food and plenty of it" was Teddy's mantra. To demonstrate, here is a menu from a dinner honoring his forty-second birthday dinner on October 27, 1900:

First Course

BLUEPOINT OYSTERS

Second Course

GREEN TURTLE SOUP, CLEAR

CELERY

OLIVES

SWEET SHERRY

Third Course

TIMBALE OF PEANUT HAM

Fourth Course

CRAB FLAKE À LA NEWBERG

Fifth Course

FILLET OF BEEF

DICKINSON GREEN PEAS

FRESH MUSHROOMS *SOUS CLOCHE* (UNDER GLASS)

Sixth Course

QUAIL & BREAD SAUCE

SALAD

ROMAN PUNCH

DESSERT CAKES & CONFECTIONERY

BISCUIT TORTONI

COFFEE & APPROPRIATE WINES WITH EACH COURSE

FDR'S FOUR ESSENTIAL FREEDOMS On January 6, 1941, war was raging in Europe and another President Roosevelt—Franklin Delano— gave a speech to Congress in which he outlined four fundamental freedoms to which humans "everywhere in the world" should be entitled:

> **The first** is freedom of speech and expression—everywhere in the world.

> **The second** is freedom of every person to worship God in his own way— everywhere in the world.

> **The third** is freedom from want—which, translated into world terms, means economic understandings which will secure to every nation a healthy peacetime life for its inhabitants—everywhere in the world.

> **The fourth** is freedom from fear—which, translated into world terms, means a worldwide reduction of armaments to such a point and in such a thorough fashion that no nation will be in a position to commit an act of physical aggression against any neighbor—anywhere in the world.

These four freedoms were adopted as war aims by the Allies as the war progressed; they were also incorporated into the preamble to the 1948 *Universal Declaration of Human Rights*.

It seems to me that the "Four Freedoms Speech" ought to be one of our nation's most recognized, but few people today seem familiar with it.

FEASTS A cultivated approach to gluttony.

FEATHER DUSTERS They make house cleaning feel more like frivolity and less like drudgery.

fig. 12: "GOLDEN LADS AND GIRLS ALL MUST, AS CHIMNEY-SWEEPERS, COME TO DUST." —*The Immortal Bard Wm. Shakespeare*

FEMMES FATALES Hollywood used to be absolutely heaving with *femmes fatales*: Louise Brooks, Rita Hayworth, Joan Bennett, and Veronica Lake, to name but a few; the great Marlene Dietrich alone was—cinematically speaking—responsible for the downfall of a veritable army of men.

Today these goddesses have been replaced with gaggles of grinning, girl-next-door "American sweethearts." One of the few genuine *femme fatale* offerings we have left—Angelina Jolie, who certainly runs with the best of them—has had to make up for that fact by practically becoming an extra-curricular Mother Teresa. Let's bring back treacherous glamour just for the fun of it.

FERN-HUNTING PARTIES People could make social events of practically *anything* in Victorian times: A once popular but now uncommon ritual was the fern-hunting party. Ferns were treasured, seminal decorating objects in Victorian homes, found in parlors, on porches, and wound into elaborate table decorations. Fronds were often framed, or pressed and saved "for use in innumerable creative ways," according to one scholar of the era's gardens.

To satisfy the Victorians' fern mania, daylong woodland excursions to procure lush new plants were frequently organized. Such outings required elaborate picnicking, of course; in between refreshments, unsuspecting ferns were uprooted and sent back to the house in baskets.

Due to the vast availability of ferns in practically every super-market in America, I suggest limiting actual fern acquisi-tion to snipping a few fronds here and there, and saving them in a journal, or—once dried and pressed—send-ing them along with lovely letters or cards.

FIGGY PUDDING If the lyrics of "We Wish You a Merry Christmas" are an accurate indicator, something about figgy pudding makes people quite bossy and demanding:

> *Oh, bring us a figgy pudding and a cup of good cheer*
> *We won't go until we get some, so bring some out here*

If it's *that* good, maybe we should bring it back. Recipes date back to the fifteenth century, but it was most popular as a Christmas dessert in the mid-nineteenth century. Here's an oldie but a goodie, unearthed from my grandmother's recipe binder. I'd never heard of a *steamed* cake before, but maybe that's the secret behind the figgy-pudding mania:

FIGGY PUDDING

1 cup suet
1 cup sugar
3 large egg yolks
1 cup milk
2 tablespoons rum
1 apple peeled, cored, and finely chopped
1 pound dried figs, ground or finely chopped
Grated peel of 1 lemon and 1 orange

1 cup chopped nuts
½ teaspoon ground cinnamon
¼ teaspoon ground cloves
¼ teaspoon ground ginger
1½ cups dried bread crumbs
2 teaspoons baking powder
3 large egg whites, stiffly beaten

Grease a two-quart mold. Cream together the butter and shortening. Gradually add the sugar, egg yolks, milk, extract, apple, figs, lemon, and orange peel. Add the next 6 ingredients, mixing well. Fold the stiffly beaten egg whites into mixture. Pour into a two-quart buttered bowl or mold and place into a large shallow pan and steam for four hours. Serve with rum sauce.

RUM SAUCE

½ cup powdered sugar
2 egg yolks
2 egg whites
3 tablespoons rum
½ cup beaten cream

Mix sugar, yolks, and rum, then the stiffly beaten whites. Cook until thick; add the beaten cream. Chill and serve.

FIGUREHEADS ON THE BOWS OF SHIPS Dating back to pre-Christian times, figureheads affixed to the prow of a ship supposedly embodied that ship's spirit and were believed to placate the gods of the sea, ensuring a safe voyage. From the sixteenth through the nineteenth centuries, practically every ship had a carved figure looking down at the waves; I don't know how today's captains *dare* face the seas without one.

FILM Most owners of digital cameras don't even make prints from their images anymore; they simply upload them to hard drives and online albums. I recently saw a photography store advertisement that declared: "The prints you make today will long outlast any computer hard drive." In this case, it was propaganda with the additional virtue of being true. I love looking at old family photo albums; but who wants to inherit Granny's hard drive?

If you *are* print-minded, my photographer friends tell me that film images are simply more lush and beautiful than digital ones. Plus, with film you get that delightful anticipation period as you wait to relive whatever event you documented, whether a wedding, a voyage, or a naughty Sunday afternoon in bed.

FINGERBOWL CHAMPAGNE GLASSES Also known as champagne coupes. They are very Fitzgeraldian; common champagne flutes, by comparison, feel rather 1980s and invoke all sorts of *Working Girl* office party imagery.

Legend has it that the shape of the champagne coupe glass was modeled on the breasts of Marie Antoinette or one of a variety of other French aristocrats, including Madame du Pompadour and Madame du Barry. At other times, the shape is attributed to Helen of Troy; supposedly her lover, Paris, made wax molds of the glorious breasts that "launched a thousand ships" and used the molds to make drinking glasses. None of these rumors is likely true, but who cares? The *idea* is enough: It emphasizes the decadent sensuality with which fine champagne should be consumed.

FINGER LOOP CIGARETTE HOLDERS If you smoke, use a finger loop cigarette holder, like Norma Desmond's in *Sunset Boulevard*. It's simply a little device with a loop on one end that you slip over your forefinger; there's a little attached shaft, and on top of that, another loop where you stick the cigarette. You must use it *only* when you're indolently lounging on an overstuffed sofa next to a dance floor, or on a veranda overlooking a bay.

FINGERNAIL BUFFING Buffing is quite elegant for both men and women—far more so than the gangrenous green and I've-been-dead-for-a-week blue polishes lining the walls of manicure salons today.

FIVE-AND-DIME STORES One of the great joys of childhood, when you usually only have nickels and dimes to spend.

SOME OF THE ORIGINAL GREAT AMERICAN FIVE-AND-DIMES,
MANY OF WHICH CROPPED UP AT THE TURN OF THE LAST CENTURY:

Woolworth's

W. T. Grant

J. J. Newberry's

McCrory's

Kresge (which later became K-Mart)

McClellan's

Ben Franklin Stores

Of these, only the Ben Franklin Stores still exist in five-and-dime form, although they've now been upgraded to "dollar" stores.

See also FAKE VOMIT *and* WAX LIPS

FLAMING WALL TORCHES Transylvania-style. Affixed to your dining room walls, they could lend gravitas to a frozen TV dinner.

FLEA CIRCUSES Until the 1930s, flea circuses epitomized absurd whimsy as sideshow attractions, in which fleas performed (or appeared to perform) all sorts of circus acts; visitors peered down at these tiny performers through magnifying lenses. One of the most famous Victorian flea circus performances was the "Extraordinary Exhibition of the Industrious Fleas" by L. Bertolotto (sometimes described as the "Andrew Lloyd Webber of Flea-biz"). It featured fleas that danced, played instruments, and pulled tiny chariots.

The wife of one famous flea circus artist allegedly made him wear a flea collar to bed.

[plate 6]

Tiniest Show on Earth

FLIP BOOKS Popular in the late 1800s, a flip book's tiny pages contained a series of pictures that varied gradually from one page to the next, so that when the pages were "flipped" or thumbed through rapidly, the pictures appeared to animate. Because they were like primitive (very) short films, they were also sometimes called "flick books." Often marketed to children, they usually featured simple motions, such as a dog leaping through a hoop or a cow jumping over the moon.

Despite the comparatively sophisticated technology that surrounds us today, these simple books are still novel and even magical, perhaps because they make a usually inanimate object come to life.

"FLIP" RINGS These pieces of jewelry were mainstay accessories in the Victorian wardrobe. During the day, you would wear the demure pastel cameo side facing up; to adorn your dinner ensemble, you'd flip over the ring's second face, which was set on a swivel and often made from onyx with a diamond or another precious stone embedded in the middle. A lavish adornment, but also very practical too—and Americans have always loved getting two things for the price of one.

"FLOOZY" Another one of those wonderful words that sounds like what it means—although I think it should have at least two or three more *o*'s in the middle.

FLORIDA WATER Obscure but still obtainable, lemony Florida water was once used as a "splash" and a perfume, and comes in a very florally charming bottle, according to the company, which says that it has used the same ingredients since 1808. The resultant potion is apparently "cooling for headaches, invigorating after exercise, [and] helpful for jangled nerves," according to one of its vendors.

FLOWERS AS A HAIR ADORNMENT The most becoming accessory of all, and yet these days we usually only wear flowers in our hair for weddings. Let's revive them for other occasions as well: cocktail parties, dinners, premieres—anything and everything. If you need convincing, look up photos of Billie Holiday with those magnificent gardenias tucked behind her ears: devastating, innocent, and sensual all at once. Men don't forget a first encounter with a woman who wears flowers in this manner.

The Victorians—who adorned themselves with flowers like crazy—came up with a smart way to keep blooms looking fresh throughout even the lengthiest ball or garden party: They created stem-shaped glass tubes filled with water, which they would then seal with wax around the stem. The tubes would be hidden in a lady's hair or a gentleman's lapel. Today's florists use similar tubes to deliver boxed flowers; keep one around next time you get a delivery and seal up the top with Blu-Tack when you adorn your tresses with fat red roses.

FLOWER-INSPIRED NAMES According to a 1900 census, names such as Rose, Myrtle, Iris, Daisy, and Flora were among the most popular baby names for American girls; by 2008, some of these names had plummeted off the census altogether.

I was very disappointed to learn that, according to the same census, my favorite flower name of all time, Petunia, was popular neither then nor now.

fig. 13: INTRINSICALLY PURE *and* LOVELY

TO: *Daisy*

With all my love
on your birthday

FLY-IN MOVIE THEATERS We all know about American drive-in movie theaters, but I'm willing to bet that you've never heard of the *fly-in* theater phenomenon. The first such establishment was reportedly opened in 1948 by a former navy pilot named Ed Brown Jr.; inspired by the growth spurt being enjoyed by the drive-in industry, he came up with the idea of courting customers with small private planes to capitalize on Americans' midcentury love affair with aviation. His Wall Township, New Jersey, fly-in could accommodate twenty-five small planes and helicopters and five hundred cars; unfortunately, the enterprise fizzled, leaving today's private plane owners to languish in regular movie theaters.

Despite the general outlandishness of the concept, it still sounds like a grand night out to me; someone *must* revive the fly-in.

FLYSWATTERS Avid use of them might bring about bad karma, but they're still very satisfying to wield. The old-fashioned "screen" ones are hard to come by these days; the only ones you can find in the hardware store now are made from ugly, heavy plastic and look like they could kill a hog. I recently found an old-guard one online. Funnily enough, the flies *knew* when the package arrived; when I opened it and laid the swatter on the table, they simply *vanished*.

FORGET-ME-NOTS It's ironic that these wistfully named little blue flowers have been largely forgotten. In the old days, a wearer believed that the blooms protected him or her from being forgotten by his or her lover. As you can imagine, *lots* of people used to wear them. Lots of people still should.

FORMALITY America seems on a quest to become ever more casual. Today's weddings and funerals often resemble business-casual conventions; people sometimes even wear pajama bottoms on planes. Even in New York City's most fashionable circles, people often can't be bothered to wear tuxedos and gowns to black-tie events anymore. Formality has its own pleasures, and its practitioners need not apologize for it. It's nice once in a while to spoil your dinner guests — or just yourself — with silver and china, or to dress up for the opera, or to drink from a crystal glass instead of a can, for heaven's sake.

fig. 14: MAKE A MARK *of* DISTINCTION

FOUNTAIN PENS Plastic ballpoint pens are so miserly; *never* sign an important document with cheap ink, especially a contract. The deal will go sour, believe me.

NO. 4711 ORIGINAL EAU DE COLOGNE Every-one made such a fuss when Calvin Klein created CK One, a perfume that could be worn by both men and women, but 4711 preempted this concept by about two hundred years. The manufacturers of 4711 have closely guarded the precise formula for the scent since the 1700s, which contains "a blend of citrus, rosemary, and other proprietary ingredients," according to one of its vendors. It comes in a gorgeous little bottle with a gold, black, and turquoise label; it's cheap as chips; and has the additional benefit of being Holly Golightly's perfume of choice.

fig. 15: A HINT *of* GRAPEFRUIT TAKES OFF TEN YEARS

THE FOX THEATER One of the most spectacular movie theaters ever constructed, San Francisco's Fox Theater was reportedly called "The Last Word" when it opened in 1929. In a resolutely Deco-dominated architec-tural era, the theater's owners, Mr. and Mrs. William Fox, created a lavishly Baroque monument with more than 4,500 seats. Other periods were also referenced: "The ladies lounge might have been a boudoir at Versailles; the gentlemen's equivalent would have made a splendid ballroom for an English Georgian country house," wrote architectural historian Constance Greiff. A pair of vases displayed there had once belonged to the last czar of Russia; Mrs. Fox apparently spent two years prior to the theater's opening scouring Europe for such ornaments.

The theater suffered financial difficulties in subsequent decades; it was demolished in 1963 and replaced with an ugly skyscraper called Fox Plaza.

FRANCS And other distinct European currencies. The bills were so beautiful and truly made you feel like you were passing from one culture into another.

Bear in mind that this is an aesthetic argument, not an economic one.

FRANKLIN, BENJAMIN (1706–1790) America's answer to Leonardo da Vinci, and a *most* admirable bon vivant.

FREAK SHOWS These days, there are frustratingly few places where one can glimpse bearded ladies, conjoined lambs, and the like. The next best thing: a curiosities shop called Evolution in New York City, which showcases all sorts of peculiar taxidermy and other earthly remains—including an astonishing array of human skulls and jarred creatures preserved in turquoise-hued alcohol. Not for the faint of heart.

THE FRIAR TUCK HAIRDO Named after the once-famous coif of Friar Tuck (one of Robin Hood's "Merry Men"), this usually-by-default 'do resembles an inner tube of hair wrapped around a man's head, with a shining bald crown peeking through at the top. It would be nice to see someone sport the Friar Tuck unapologetically. Not only is it endearingly self-deprecating, it performs a public service: providing the masses with a much-needed laugh.

See also TOUPEES

FRIENDSHIP PINS An elementary-school pleasure: little girls used to line the shanks of safety pins with tiny colored beads and gift them to their friends, who would in turn attach them to their shoelaces for the world to see. The different colors meant different things: an all-yellow pin stood for affection, but all-green ones brought about unhappy results (they implied jealousy, as did green M&Ms).

FRINGE On lamps, settees, couches, chairs, curtain edges—fringe on *everything*. It instantly upgrades plain or humble furniture and provides a boudoirish, 1930s counterpoint to the stark, unadorned lines of modern furniture.

"FRIPPERY" A perfectly wonderful old word meaning clothing that is "showy," "gaudy," or "tawdry"; it also means "unnecessary finery or ornament, especially in dress." Red-carpet fashion these days certainly proves that much of what passes today as "finery" is little more than "frippery."

See also ELEGANCE

FRONTIERS First we had the Wild West; then we had the moon; now we need a new one. America *needs* to pursue new frontiers in order to stay "American."

FROWSY A powdery way of calling someone or something "dumpy" or "slovenly."

FRUIT HATS Those midcentury hats brimming with cherries and grapes. The most famous fruit hat wearer was, of course, iconic samba singer and actress Carmen Miranda; her fruit turbans in the 1940s and '50s were absolutely heaped with bananas, oranges, lemons, limes, and even pineapples. A stylish approach to breakfast-on-the-run.

FUR MUFFS *Doctor Zhivago* chic. Perhaps a little too costumey when paired with a matching hat, but the epitome of luxury when worn with a slender cashmere coat.

FUR SHAG RUGS Aptly named: They are synonymous with making *lovvvvve*. In fact, in the 1970s, it was apparently impossible to have relations when *not* in the presence of a fur shag rug.

G

GAME NIGHT Scrabble, Bridge, Poker, Battleship, Trivial Pursuit, Monopoly: Game nights used to serve as wonderful occasions to get soused and gossip.

GARBO, GRETA (1905–1990) Her biographers often make her sound like a manipulative joy suck, but one can't deny that she was profoundly photogenic. Two aspects of Garbo's particular sort of beauty are especially rare today, and should be appreciated by modern women:

> **I. HER NATURAL-LOOKING, SLENDER LIPS.** Garbo has been long lauded by plastic surgeons for embodying facial perfection, based on the symmetry of her famous features. If you look closely, you'll notice that her lips are slender by today's standards, and she never did anything to alter their shape, cosmetically or surgically. In fact, you rarely (if ever) see photos of her sporting the heavily stylized, dark, "cupid's bow" lipstick line so popular in the silent-film era; in portraits, Garbo's lipstick always follows the natural contours of her mouth.

> The world's most perfect lips are a far cry from the needle-induced, duck-mouth, pillow-lip aesthetic so rampant today; it would be much less painful and expensive for all of us if the Garbo-lip contour came back into fashion.

> **2. THE SIMPLICITY OF HER ROUTINE.** Garbo's at-home beauty arsenal reportedly resembled that of a nun, consisting of "a single toothbrush, a comb missing several teeth, and half a bar of Lux soap," according to Old Hollywood biographer Diana McLellan. I don't know how *anyone* could tolerate such extreme spareness; yet the contents of Garbo's bathroom offer a good lesson: If this timeless Aphrodite didn't rely on heaps of dubious and costly beauty products, we probably don't need to either.

GARÇONNIÈRES Why on *earth* did these go out of style? Most frequently described as a "bachelor's residence," a *garçonnière* is a little house built for teenage boys and young men alongside the family's main residence. *Garçonnières* give parents privacy, and boys get to do all of the delightfully filthy things they like to do when alone. Everyone's happy.

There are several surviving examples of these ingenious structures at some antebellum homes around New Orleans: The San Francisco Plantation in Louisiana has wonderful *garçonnières* that look like silos or dovecotes.

THE "GARDEN OF ALLAH" This famous Sunset Boulevard mansion became notorious in the 1920s for the wild parties held by its owner, flamboyant screen actress Alla Nazimova. The large Spanish-Moorish house sported an aviary, a veritable forest of citrus trees and bougainvillea, and an underlit swimming pool supposedly shaped like the Black Sea, although you probably had to be really drunk to see the resemblance.

When her once-illustrious career declined, Nazimova decided to turn her grounds into a hotel of sorts; she built a complex of twenty-five small bungalows ("villas" she called them) around the Black Sea, and, according to legend, honored the establishment's opening with an eighteen-hour fete, which every Hollywood heavyweight attended. Over the years, famous Garden of Allah tenants included Marlene Dietrich, F. Scott Fitzgerald (who reportedly wrote himself a postcard while there: "Dear Scott—How are you? Have been meaning to come in and see you. I have living [sic] at the Garden of Allah Yours Scott Fitzgerald"), Ernest Hemingway, Fanny Brice, Laurence Olivier, Orson Welles, Humphrey Bogart, Dorothy Parker, Errol Flynn, and Greta Garbo.

Today's decadent party hotel in Los Angeles, the Chateau Marmont, likely couldn't hold a candle to the volume of liquor consumed, drugs taken, fistfights, sexual liaisons of all varieties, and other decadent hedonisms of the Garden of Allah. "Nothing interrupted the continual tumult that was life at the Garden of Allah," the columnist Lucius Beebe once told *Time* magazine. "Now and then the men in white came with a van and took somebody away, . . . [but] nobody paid any mind."

Yet all wild parties eventually dissolve into lurid hangovers: While it likely should have been landmarked, the Garden was demolished in 1959. What's there now: a strip mall and parking lot. People scarf down Subway hoagies on the sacred site, instead of luxuriating among lemon trees, hummingbirds, and the ghosts of Old Hollywood's stars.

GARDEN PARTIES These have, in recent years, been supplanted by their honky-tonk cousin, the modern barbeque. Garden parties are very easy and pretty: Pass out cucumber sandwiches and macaroons, fill punch bowls with icy lemonade or something stronger (also see "Whirligig Punch"), ask the ladies to wear wide-brimmed hats and the men to wear straw fedoras. The loveliest moment: when a successful garden party yawns into the twilight hour and the lightning bugs start to come out. Everyone looks beautiful in this poignant light.

GARGOYLES And grotesques. The difference: Gargoyles spout water, grotesques do not.

See also ANIMAL-SHAPED TOPIARIES

GARTER BELTS They looked sexy and felt sexy. Getting into a pair of modern pantyhose, on the other hand, always feels akin to mashing tooth-paste back into the tube.

GASLIT STREETLAMPS Look up Robert Doisneau's photographs of 1940s and '50s Paris, or visit the quieter pockets of New Orleans' French Quarter if you need to be reminded how romantic gaslit streetlamps are.

GELLHORN, MARTHA (1908–1998) Among America's earliest female war correspondents, Gellhorn covered nearly every major conflict between the Spanish Civil War and the end of the Cold War. She also briefly married writer Ernest Hemingway, but her supreme independence and his supreme egotism proved a bad match. When she left him behind in Cuba to cover World War II in Europe, Hemingway regaled her with petulant cables, including one that read: "Are you a war correspondent or wife in my bed?"

I think you can surmise her response.

GEMSTONE ENGAGEMENT RINGS

Today's large diamond companies have heavily marketed the necessity of showing one's love for your soon-to-be betrothed through a diamond and a diamond alone; yet there is something wonderful about Victorian-era nondiamond gemstone engagement rings. Let's bring back fiery, neon-flecked opals; clear aquamarines the size of skipping stones; delicately domed turquoise; and deep-blue sapphires to adorn our beloveds' ring fingers instead of the tried-but-tired diamond engagement ring. Of course, there's no need to oust the diamonds altogether—just heavily lace the borders of the other precious gems with old mine-cut diamonds for a dose of sparkle and modern tradition.

—*Lisa Salzer* • DESIGNER, LULU FROST JEWELRY

GENERATIONAL HOUSES In other words, houses that are passed down through generations of the same family. An architect recently told me that today's Americans dwell in the same domicile for an average of just three to five years.

THE GENEVA CONVENTIONS These international laws—which set the standards for humanitarian treatment of prisoners of war—have been somewhat shunted aside these past few years: This is not exactly a great vote of confidence for human nature.

GEORGE MAGAZINE I loved this magazine, but apparently I was one of only a few who did; it closed in 2001 after a six-year run. As the son of JFK Sr., the magazine's founder, John F. Kennedy Jr., knew from personal family history that politics and sex often go together like peanut butter and jelly; he was way ahead of his time in creating a mainstream publication that linked the political, entertainment, and media worlds. *George* foreshadowed the tenor of *Talk* magazine (1999–2002), as well as the *Daily Beast* and a myriad of other similar Web sites and publications.

TEXT CONTINUES NEXT PAGE ⟫→

While we're at it, let's bring back John F. Kennedy Jr. as well. As his former Brown University housemate, reporter Christiane Amanpour, once reportedly said, "He was an exquisite hunk, a perfect ten." Not to mention a heartbreaking emblem of unfulfilled potential, like so many other members of his clan.

GHOULISH NURSERY SONGS Like many classic children's stories, many beloved old children's nursery songs had gruesome undertones and content. Not that kids have ever minded such morbidity; as one astute author once said to me, "Fear is like sex for kids."

SOME EXAMPLES:

- • • "**SING A SONG OF SIXPENCE**" contains a line in which "a little blackbird" swoops in and snaps off a maid's nose; in some versions of the song, the king's doctor sews it back on.

- • • "**ROCK-A-BYE BABY**" (originally called "Hush-a-Bye Baby") features an infant falling, cradle and all, from a treetop.

- • • THE "**RING AROUND THE ROSIE**" (or "Ring a Ring o' Roses") line "ashes, ashes, we all fall down" refers to the Black Plague, when people were dropping like flies and their bodies tossed onto pyres to keep the disease from spreading further.

- • • "**THE TITANIC SONG**," often sung at camps, contains a particularly harrowing passage, in which "Little children wept and cried, as the waves rushed o'er the side."

GHOST LIGHTS A wonderful theater tradition: a single bare-bulb, freestanding light left burning on a deserted stage overnight. The practical explanation: It prevented after-hours injuries among any late-staying stagehands. The whimsical explanation: It warded off ghosts.

GILT-EDGED BOOK PAGES It's an expensive flourish, so sadly, most books these days have to go without.

Speaking of going without, after squandering an enormous fortune, Italian heiress Luisa Casati was left with only a smattering of belongings to remember her glory years: a broken cuckoo clock, a stuffed lion's head, and a purported fragment of St. Peter's finger that had once been "flung at her during a séance," according to a biographer. She had also been able to keep a few books from a once-vast collection and displayed them with the gilt-edged pages facing outward, making a regular row of volumes appear to be a block of shining gold.

GIMLETS Once a very popular drink, the straight-ahead gimlet has been occluded in recent years by the scourge of saccharine cosmopolitans and fruit-flavored martinis. A simple 1930s gimlet recipe (a "jigger" is a 1½ ounce whiskey shot glass):

GIMLET	½ jigger Burrough's Plymouth Gin ½ jigger Rose's Lime Juice Cordial
	Stir and serve in a glass over ice.

There are various theories about the drink's origin, but most sources agree that the British Royal Navy likely created the drink in the 1870s, when the United Kingdom mandated daily lime juice rations to every merchant fleet sailor to stave off scurvy (a disease caused by Vitamin C deficiency). One source reports that Rose's lime juice cordial was actually invented for the navy for this exact purpose. At some point, it became a fashionable ladies' libation as well—and was a great favorite of many Southern *grandes dames*, along with mint juleps and absinthe.

THE ORIGINAL GIRL SCOUT COOKIES Packaged Girl Scout Cookies have been big business for decades. While those Thin Mints and Samoas are addictive, there is something endearing about the original sugar cookies peddled by the earliest Girl Scouts—which were reportedly the most delicious Girl Scout cookies of all. In the 1920s and '30s, Girl Scouts and their mothers cooked their own cookies from the following official recipe; they then packaged these simple goodies in wax paper bags, sealed them with a sticker, and sold the bags door to door for twenty-five to thirty-five cents per dozen.

GIRL SCOUT COOKIES

1 cup butter
1 cup sugar plus additional amount for topping
2 eggs
2 tablespoons milk
1 teaspoon vanilla
2 cups flour
1 teaspoon salt
2 teaspoons baking powder

Cream butter and the cup of sugar; add well-beaten eggs, then milk, vanilla, flour, salt, and baking powder. Refrigerate for at least 1 hour. Roll dough, cut into trefoil shapes, and sprinkle sugar on top, if desired. Bake in a quick oven (375 degrees F) for approximately 8 to 10 minutes or until the edges begin to brown. Makes six- to seven-dozen cookies.

—FROM GIRL SCOUT PUBLICATION
THE AMERICAN GIRL, VOLUME V, NUMBER 10, JULY 1922

GLAMOUR SLIPPERS The ultimate house shoe: a befeathered, silken, froufrou alternative to slapping, schlumpy flip-flops.

See also BONBONS

THE GLASS FAMILY Iconic, recently deceased author J. D. Salinger was best known for his 1951 novel *The Catcher in the Rye*, but equally fascinating are his stories centered on the fictional Glass family, composed of seven precocious, often-troubled ex-child star siblings who once appeared on a radio quiz show called *It's a Wise Child*. "I love working on these Glass stories," Salinger once wrote. "I've been waiting for them most of my life."

THE SEVEN GLASS CHILDREN ARE:

Seymour Glass

Webb Gallagher "Buddy" Glass

Beatrice "Boo Boo" Glass Tannenbaum

Walter "Walt" Glass

Waker Glass (twin to Walter)

Zachary Martin "Zooey" Glass

Frances "Franny" Glass

AND SOME OF THE STORIES IN WHICH THEY APPEAR OR ARE REFERENCED:

"A Perfect Day for Bananafish" (*The New Yorker*, 1948)

"Uncle Wiggily in Connecticut" (*The New Yorker*, 1948)

"Down at the Dinghy" (*Harper's*, 1949)

"Franny" (*The New Yorker*, 1955)

"Raise High the Roof Beam, Carpenters" (*The New Yorker*, 1955)

"Zooey" (*The New Yorker*, 1957)

"Seymour: An Introduction" (*The New Yorker,* 1959)

"Hapworth 16, 1924" (*The New Yorker*, 1965)

Buddy Glass—who narrates "Raise High the Roof Beam, Carpenters" and "Seymour: an Introduction," and appears in other stories—is considered by many scholars and readers to *be* Salinger himself masquerading under a pseudonym. Salinger did little to discourage this impression, writing once: "I work like greased lightning, myself, but my alter ego and collaborator, Buddy Glass, is insufferably slow." Biographers will likely long comb through Buddy's musings as a window into the reclusive Salinger's mind.

GLASSES ON MEN Few men today wear glasses compared to just a few decades ago; everyone has switched to contact lenses. While there are obvious benefits to lenses, men have lost yet another defining accessory (along with pocket watches, hats, and so on); what's more, glasses look *good* on most men: They're very face-framing, brainy-looking, and very *Mad Men* chic.

fig. 16: SIP
VOLUPTUOUSLY

GOBLETS Some retailers today market wine goblets, but the prevalent word for such items is wine "glasses." While they may be exactly the same item, I contend that you enjoy wine from a goblet *far* more than wine swilled from a common old glass. The word *goblet* implies regal gluttony, and evokes bacchanalian or medieval feasts, at which you eat meat with your hands and get up to all sorts of naughtiness afterward. Bacchus himself would surely approve of the word's return.

GOLD TEETH So festive. Also: handy assets in a recession.

GOOD CRACKERJACK PRIZES These days, the ones inside those hallowed boxes of caramelized popcorn are *pitiful*.

"GOOD" SALUTATIONS As in "Good morning" and "Good night": Let's revive the whole range, including "Good day," "Good afternoon," and "Good evening." Speakers of the romance languages still use all of these phrases; they sound just as mannerly in English.

GOSSIP We need to have at least *one* vice these days, now that we're being cured of all of our other ones.

GOVERNESSES Much more distinctive than a regular old nanny. Pop lit of recent years has cast the nanny as a browbeaten doormat; the governess, however, retains her regal bearing, thanks to Wharton and writers of her epoch.

"GRAND" Instead of "Grandma," Jacqueline Kennedy Onassis was known to her grandchildren as "Grand Jackie." I'm surprised that Marlene Dietrich—who was eventually forced to transition from a lifelong sex symbol to "the world's most famous grandmother"—didn't come up with this image-preserving honorific first.

THE "GRAND TOUR" A practice in which wealthy nineteenth- and early-twentieth-century American families embarked on monthslong grand excursions through Europe. The family would take in the sights of the major capitals and resorts: London, Paris, Rome, Venice, Florence, Lausanne, Athens, Munich, and so on; young Grand Tourists would expand their horizons, pick up some languages, and come back home as sophisticated as could be.

That said, the old Grand Tour wasn't *all* about ennobling the youth with education and perspective: Sometimes Grand Tourists would pick up an impoverished aristocrat for the eldest daughter along the way. They'd often also return to America with the contents of several stripped-down Old World palaces to furnish their New World palaces in places like Newport, Detroit, Chicago, New York, or Palm Beach.

It couldn't hurt to repopularize some version of these trips; Americans are always being accused by foreigners of being provincial.

THE GRAND UNION HOTEL This beautiful Gilded Age hotel in Saratoga Springs, New York, became an emblem of the elite racing culture of the era. While a less posh destination than Newport, Saratoga Springs was also a prominent playground for the supremely wealthy; the two pleasure centers are often mentioned in the same breath. Edith Wharton aptly described the setting and this culture in her unfinished novel *The Buccaneers*, which features a hotel that strongly resembles the old Grand Union. Saratoga Springs and its racetracks went out of style in the early twentieth century; with no bustled-and-corseted patrons left to social climb within its walls, the Grand Union was demolished in 1953.

GRANDES DAMES If they occupied a hallowed part of society again, it would give us women something to look forward to.

GRANDFATHER CLOCKS Their chimes keep you company on nights when you have insomnia.

GRASSHOPPERS This mint-flavored after-dinner drink will refresh you and knock you flat on your back at the same time. Reportedly invented by Tujague's, a landmark bar in New Orleans, the grasshopper was wildly popular in the 1950s and '60s. You can add ice cream if you want to feel slightly more wholesome about things.

GRASSHOPPER

3 ounces white crème de cacao
3 ounces green crème de menthe
2 ounces heavy cream or
½ cup vanilla ice cream (or more)
½ cup crushed ice

Blend in blender until smooth.

GRAVESTONES As if the act of dying isn't insulting enough, so many people today get to look forward to weathering eternity under one of those hideous, chunky, speckled faux marble slabs cluttering up graveyards today. Someday I hope to reside permanently under a beautiful nineteenth-century-style tablet gravestone of thin white marble, with all sorts of scrollwork; my mother has requested a rather elaborate tomb (an obelisk simply won't do). In previous eras, tombstones of children—always a wrenching sight—were crested with carvings of sleeping lambs and other consoling animals; sometimes a headstone would feature an enameled portrait of the grave's occupant. Always pretty: a carving of praying hands, usually above the words "Gone Home."

See also EPITAPHS

[PLATE 7]

Here Lies My Beloved

"A GREAT BEAUTY" This phrase is usually followed by the words, "in her day." I like it because it suggests beauty of a strong variety.

GREEK CHORUSES Especially for those of us with impulse-control issues, the Greek choruses of yore might come in handy as modern deterrents: they could warn us when we're recklessly about to overdraw our checking accounts or engage in other preventable catastrophes.

GREEK REVIVAL ARCHITECTURE FOR BANKS In the nineteenth century, many American banks built weighty Greek Revival headquarters to give wary would-be customers the impression of solidity and grandeur. God knows American banks are in need of an image boost these days; maybe Ionic or Doric columns would help.

GREEN ACCOUNTANT VISORS Going to the accountant can be such a demoralizing ritual; it would be nicer if they could give us something colorful to look at.

GRIDDLECAKES Cake for breakfast: always a delight. Also wonderful: flapjacks.

GRIEF, PRIVATE Despite our society's current experiment in tell-all ostentation, some things are still best done behind closed doors, and grieving is one of them.

We should also refrain from prying into the grief of others—and this goes for respecting the sanctity of celebrities' tragedies as well. Keeping a courteous distance used to be considered basic good manners, and today it remains a mark of societal decency.

See also VEILS

GROCERS Altogether different from today's convenience stores. Let's bring back grocery stores, with their wood shelves, crates of vegetables, cans with vibrantly colored labels, and those beautiful old tin ceilings. If you find yourself in Manhattan's West Village sometime, pop into Myers of Keswick on Hudson Street: It has all of the delights listed above, plus a beautiful old wood-and-glass-fronted refrigerator covering the entire back wall.

GUEST BOOKS These blank books would lie open on a table in the front foyer; guests to the house would sign their names, the date of their visit, the occasion, and any comments or thoughts. The guest book became a house diary, recording all of the comings and goings; the signatures inside composed a vivid photograph album of sorts.

See also PENMANSHIP

"GUNG HO" This fun old term, meaning "wholeheartedly enthusiastic," originally came from the Chinese term gonghe. It was picked up and "slangified" in the early 1940s by Carlson's Raiders, a World War II guerrilla unit operating in the Pacific theater. It's funny how these things trickle down from the most unlikely sources into our vernacular, and then right back out again.

GYPSIES The campy, roaming-the-countryside and fortune-telling variety, as portrayed by Marlene Dietrich in *Golden Earrings* (1947). Fetchingly smudged with dirt, draped in a burlap head scarf, coins dangling from her bracelets and earlobes, Dietrich was indeed, as her daughter later said, "the gypsiest gypsy that ever was."

See also SUPERSTITIONS

HAIRDRESSERS Much chicer than going to see a "stylist." I've always liked the idea of hair getting dressed along with the rest of you.

HAIR POWDER It used to be widely used, along with dry shampoos. You'd spray the powder lightly onto your unwashed tendrils; it would dutifully soak up any oil, and *presto*—you'd be out the door.

HAIR "RATS" Admittedly a poor choice of name, yet the object itself was rather refined and very useful, especially to ladies with fine hair. Once personal boudoir and salon mainstays, hair rats were thick doughnut- or roll-shaped nylon mesh forms that you used to create fuller hair buns; you'd get one that matched your hair color and wrap your tendrils around it artfully; suddenly it would appear that your hair was twice as thick (or twice as high—very important in the 1960s).

HAND MIRRORS For centuries, women had vanity table "toilette sets," which usually included a lovely matching hairbrush and hand mirror. Expensive evening purses also used to contain compartments sewn into the lining that contained the following: a change purse made from the lining material (often silk or satin), a comb, and a small hand mirror, sometimes with a little prop on the back so you could stand it up on the table and refresh your lipstick.

HANDLEBAR MUSTACHES ON BARTENDERS You'd need very little additional decor in the bar.

"HANDSOME" To describe men and women alike. I've also seen women delightfully described in old debutante announcements as "ornamental."

HANDWRITTEN THANK-YOU NOTES Supposedly it's the thought that counts, but an e-mailed thank-you note hints at shortcutting. According to manners experts, thank-you notes should be sent within twenty-four hours of receiving a gift or attending a dinner or other social occasion; brides and grooms, however, get a three-month grace period in sending thank-you notes for wedding gifts.

HANGING WICKER RATTAN SWING CHAIRS An egg-shaped 1970s delight; better inside than on the porch. It's always fun to have a couch on the lawn and a swing in the living room.

HANKIES To help you look more contrite and convincing on the witness stand.

HAT BOXES Especially romantic when used as hand luggage on a train journey.

HATS Everyone seems to want hats to stage a big comeback, but no one is willing to take the first step of wearing them consistently. Let's be bold and take the plunge together; as designer Christian Dior once advised, "Women would be very silly not to take advantage of such an efficient weapon of coquetry."

Hats used to truly complete an outfit—and during some eras they were the most important items in a woman's wardrobe; they remain an easy way to add an elegant, dramatic, or amusing flourish; in fact, you can get away with a murderously boring outfit if a clever hat is perched on your crown. They also mask a bad hair day and save you a trip to the shower if you can't be bothered.

Men also look gorgeous and debonair in hats; there was a time when no self-respecting man would leave the house without one. Let's revive a wide array for the chaps: fedoras, boaters, porkpies, newsboy caps—but baseball caps *certainly* do not count.

[PLATE 8]

a barman of Visibly Virile character

HAVANA Once one of the most celebrated pleasure centers on the planet. Despite its sequestered erosion, there's something damn evocative about how it's been suspended at the pinnacle of its heyday, with those faded pastel facades and 1950s cars everywhere.

HAYSTACKS One always sees hay crammed into those drearily efficient rolls these days. Old-guard, haphazard haystacks just look romantic; one imagines roaming gypsies sleeping in them at night. Until farmers see the error of their ways in this regard, we have Monet's haystack series to tide us over.

HEAD, EDITH (1897–1981) Legendary costume designer, Ms. Head— a.k.a. the "Dress Doctor"—was as glamorous as the stars she dressed, and she dressed countless major Old Hollywood stars in some of their most memorable roles. If you loved Grace Kelly's iconic look in *Rear Window* or Audrey Hepburn's lavish wardrobe in *Funny Face,* one of Hollywood's ultimate fashion movies, take your hat off to Edith. The winner of eight Oscars (she was nominated for *thirty-four*), Ms. Head also had a heavy appetite for glamour and absolutely *heaped* it on the stars of *Sunset Boulevard, All About Eve*, and more than four hundred other films. On the flamboyance of the times, Ms. Head once described Old Hollywood as a "Barnum & Bailey World," filled with gold bathtubs, ermine bathrobes, and film actresses draped in satins and minks. "I caught the flavor and the fever," she recalled.

Ms. Head's snippets of advice and witticisms were as closely heeded as those attributed to Coco Chanel, and they remain relevant today:

- • • "You can have anything you want in life if you dress for it."
- • • "Life is competition; clothes gird us for the competition."
- • • "The cardinal sin is not being badly dressed, but wearing the right thing in the wrong place."
- • • "Your dresses should be tight enough to show you're a woman and loose enough to prove you're a lady."
- • • "Clothes not only can make the woman; they can make her several different women."
- • • "I say sacrifice style any day for becomingness."

HEAD SCARVES Very Jackie-Kennedy-and-Lee-Radziwill-in-Capri; an excellent alternative to pulling your hair back into a stringy, drab ponytail. Head scarves are also a good way to keep your hair from getting stringy while you're zipping around in a convertible.

"HEAVE-HO" As in, "give him the ol' heave-ho." The phrase implies the removal of an enormous weight, which is usually the case.

HEAVYWEIGHT BOXING I often hear men complain that boxing just isn't what it was in the era of George Foreman, Muhammad Ali, and "Smokin' Joe" Frazier; they mutter something about how there are too many belts and divisions today. While this is not a world I know a lot about, I know that it means a great deal to a great many: So let's bring back a system that produces meaningful champions.

HEDGE MAZES In an era in which your cell phone acts as a homing device and you're "Never Lost" thanks to GPS systems—it might be nice to go hopelessly astray for an afternoon in a tall topiary labyrinth. Hedge mazes were very popular in the palaces and grand houses of Europe up through the eighteenth century, when they started to fall out of fashion; later incarnations fell into disrepair or died during the First and Second World Wars. The United Kingdom's Hampton Court Palace's hornbeam maze, planted around 1690 to mark the arrival of William III (of Orange) in England, is thought to be the oldest surviving one in the world.

HEIRLOOMS In previous eras, newly married couples were often given family china, silver, and crystal as wedding gifts; however, I was recently told by a luxury-goods expert that today's obediently consumerist brides "want nothing to do with Granny's china."

HIEROGLYPHICS They're great for cryptic love letters to crushes.

HIGHBALLS Actually, we still have highballs aplenty: We just don't call them that anymore. By definition, a highball is simply a mixed drink composed of an alcoholic base spirit and a larger proportion of a nonalcoholic mixer. It just sounds more dignified to order a "highball" than a "Jack and Coke."

fig. 17: NEVER MIX, NEVER WORRY

HIRED MOURNERS Those ample women who shriek and wail and beat their breasts in grief. *Someone* has to cry at funerals these days; the affairs have become altogether too casual. People can barely be bothered to wear *black* anymore, often donning instead the sensible outfit they wore to a business conference the week before.

HOBBIES Today's children don't get to have hobbies; instead, they get "extracurricular activities." Let's bring back classic pastimes for them: model airplane building, train sets, junior chemistry sets, scrapbook making. And collections: stamps, stickers, coins, books, beads, baseball cards, and butterflies.

HOBBY HORSES Along with rocking horses, hobby horses provide an early taste of the Wild West without the inconveniences of frontier living. Best served with a cowboy hat or a Laura Ingalls Wilder–style sunbonnet.

"HOLIDAY" The word "vacation" sounds bureaucratic. "Holiday" sounds like fun.

HOME CONSERVATORIES These glass-walled and -ceilinged, palm-, orchid-, and fern-filled, attached-to-the-house greenhouses remind me of reverse zoos: For once, nature gets to observe humans in their domiciles.

HOME-DELIVERED MILK AND SELTZER In glass bottles, of course. I'm always running out of milk, and I hate those sticky, leaky cartons. Apparently there are companies that still deliver seltzer to your house in those gorgeous old colored bottles, such as the fetchingly named Gomberg Seltzer Works in Canarsie, New York.

HOME MOVIE PROJECTORS Nothing is more poignant than Super 8mm films of birthday parties and trips to Paris played back on a flickering projector.

HOME WET BARS Homes in the 1950s and '60s often boasted full-size, practically professionally equipped wet bars—you'll recall the Robinsons' absolutely formidable bar in *The Graduate,* complete with white leather swivel chairs and enough alcohol to keep a platoon drunk for a week; people of that era took their drinking *very* seriously. Dinner party invitations called for cocktails at 6:30 or 7 and dinner at 8, leaving a good chunk of time for bonding with the booze. This is a very humane social ritual for scrambling hostesses: After more than an hour of highballs and stiff martinis, did the guests *care* what they ate? They probably couldn't even *see* the food.

HOMELY CHRISTMAS TREES Lopsided ones with fat colored lights and homemade ornaments and popcorn strings. Matchy-matchy Martha Stewart trees with white lights and red plaid ribbons look constipated.

fig. 18: A HARD WORKER

HONEYBEES According to *National Geographic,* the domesticated honeybee population has fallen by nearly half in the last fifty years. A great deal is at stake if this trend continues. The disappearance of honeybees would seriously affect our food supply: An estimated $14 billion of agricultural crops in the United States are dependent on bee pollination. Bees are also responsible for 15 to 30 percent of the food U.S. consumers eat, and unless something is done to reverse their decline, many fruits and vegetables will disappear from our tables.

"HOOLIGAN" A delightful word for a distinctly undelightful entity: "a tough and aggressive or violent youth." It first appeared in London police-court reports in 1898 and was "almost certainly [derived] from the surname Houlihan, supposedly from a lively family of that name in London who figured in music hall songs of the decade," according to Dictionary.com. Journalists picked up on the term and liked it enough to transmute it into various adjectives ("hooliganesque," "hooliganic") and a verb ("to hooligan"); other popular synonyms at the time: "lout," "ruffian," and "scofflaw."

See also WHIPPERSNAPPER

THE "HOOTCHY-KOOTCHY" DANCE The hootchy-kootchy was a burlesque version of the belly dance: a vastly underappreciated art form. And just *think* of all of the poor tassel companies that went out of business when the hootchy-kootchy lost its allure.

HOT AIR BALLOONS A wonderfully romantic way to travel. See the countryside without the annoyance of traffic; enjoy all of the benefits of altitude without vile airplane air or annoying seatmates.

Hot air balloons provided people with their first God's-eye glimpses of the earth from the sky, although the earliest passengers weren't human at all. In September 1783, scientist Jean-François Pilâtre de Rozier launched the first hot air balloon, called *Aerostat Reveillon;* inside, a sheep, a duck, and a rooster enjoyed the vista for fifteen minutes before the balloon swooped back to the ground.

HOT TODDIES The real cure for the common cold, and therefore a reasonable excuse to stay drunk all winter long. The stuff of colonial taverns (where iced cocktails were unheard of), hot toddies are very easy to make. A fairly standard recipe:

HOT TODDY

1 tablespoon honey
¾ cup tea
2 shots brandy
1 slice lemon

Brew tea and fill a tall glass ³/₄ full. Mix in honey and brandy shots, and add the lemon slice.

HOTEL DETECTIVES Also known as "house dicks." You can see why *that* term went out of fashion.

HOTEL LIVING This used to be a common practice in hotels of grandeur *and* disrepute; you would simply move into town and "take rooms." One advantage to hotel living: If you die there, you're more likely to be found in a timely manner.

SOME FAMOUS PEOPLE WHO DIED IN THEIR HOTEL DIGS:

• • • **OSCAR WILDE,** in a small, frowsy room at the Hotel d'Alsace in Paris. His reported last words: "I am dying as I have lived: beyond my means." (Other sources claim that he uttered, "Either those curtains go, or I do.")

• • • **DOROTHY PARKER,** at the Volney Hotel in New York City. Ironically, in earlier years, she loved to ridicule the culture of old hotel-dwelling ladies. The worst part: After Parker was cremated, no one collected the ashes, and her urn was stored in her lawyer's metal file cabinet for *fifteen years* before being properly interred.

• • • **EUGENE O'NEILL,** in room 401 at the Sheraton Hotel in Boston. The playwright's reported last words: "I knew it. I knew it. Born in a hotel room—goddamn it, died in a hotel room."

HOURGLASSES A less-jarring alternative to timers and alarms.

HUMILITY

There is no style without this now-rare, powerful force that pulls you into someone's space with total seduction and power.

—*Ralph Rucci* • ARTIST; HAUTE COUTURIER; DESIGNER, *CHADO RALPH RUCCI*

HULA HOOPS Talk about reinventing the wheel: The hula hoop has been making comebacks since ancient times, when the Greeks are believed to have used grapevine hoops for exercise. Around 1300, a hooping craze reportedly hit Great Britain, and homemade versions of the toy became very popular. And *then* came . . . Wham-O.

After first starting business in a garage in 1948, Wham-O's Richard Knerr and Arthur "Spud" Melin made a fortune popularizing toys based on ancient designs, such as the discus-derived Frisbee and the slingshot. In 1958, they started manufacturing a plastic hoop toy, which they trademarked the "Hula Hoop"; within four months, they'd sold twenty-five million hoops for $1.98 a pop.

The hula hoop's popularity eventually waned in the 1970s—but they are exceedingly good exercise and are overdue for their next mass revival.

I J
with

THE ICE SKATING RINK AT THE GRAND HOTEL, ST. MORITZ
Perhaps the best part of this operation was the "waiter's school" there, at which apprentice waiters learned to ice skate while carrying trays heavily laden with ice, crystal glasses, and cold champagne to the fur-clad resort guests having lunch and cocktails at the rink. Photojournalist Alfred Eisenstaedt immortalized this scene with a 1932 shot of a waiter—attired in formal tails—sailing over the ice with a glasses-covered tray, one leg extended gracefully behind him, the snow-covered Swiss mountains in the background.

ID BRACELETS Military-inspired ID bracelets became a fashionable accessory for women during World War II, when GIs gifted them to their sweethearts. By the war's end, sterling-silver ID bracelets were being advertised in magazines as "the perfect gift": Your name was engraved on the front and a private message was stamped on the back. They would make especially good gifts for authors, who are apt to forget their own names when they've been writing in isolation long enough.

IMPERFECT SMILES Today's Hollywood smiles can be downright terrifying: all of those oversize, ultrabright, über-even, deeply artificial-looking rows of teeth. Not that anyone wants to return to the aesthetics of the medieval mouth, but a slightly more natural look would be much appreciated.

A LIST OF THE OWNERS OF SOME OF AMERICA'S
FAMOUSLY IMPERFECT—AND MUCH-ADORED—SMILES:

Theodore Roosevelt	Lara Stone
David Letterman	George Foreman
Lauren Hutton	Arnold Schwarzenegger
Madonna	

IMPRACTICALITY Being practical about everything gets in the way of fun.

INDIAN PUDDING Homey bread puddings and rice puddings have made quite a comeback in New York City, and I suspect that they've never gone out of style elsewhere. But one rarely sees spicy Indian pudding on menus, which is a shame, because it can be sublime. A good recipe, once again, courtesy of my grandmother's recipe box:

INDIAN PUDDING

1 cup yellow cornmeal
4 cups milk, heated but not boiling
2 eggs, beaten
3 ounces finely minced suet
½ cup sugar
⅔ cup molasses
¾ teaspoon salt
¼ teaspoon ground ginger
⅛ teaspoon ground allspice
¼ teaspoon cinnamon
⅛ teaspoon ground nutmeg
¼ teaspoon ground cloves
⅛ teaspoon ground nutmeg

Preheat the oven to 325 degrees F; butter an eight-inch baking dish. Gradually shake the cornmeal into the milk and stir; mix until the mixture thickens. Cool slightly; fold in the beaten eggs. Add the remaining ingredients and mix well. Pour the mixture into the greased baking dish and bake for 2 hours. Serve hot with vanilla ice cream.

INDOOR TRELLIS ROOMS They bring the great outdoors inside. Trellis rooms were popularized by world-famous interior decorator Elsie de Wolfe, who in 1905 created a magnificent green trellis-lined room in New York's famous Colony Club; it was designed to give the Club's ladies the sensation of being in a formal outdoor tea garden. This is an especially clever decorating trick for today's urban dwellers; so many of us live *sans* private outdoor space and don't even have window boxes. Place planters at the feet of the indoor trellises and tease ivy or passionflower vines up the walls.

[PLATE 9]

Smile and the world smiles with you

THE INSULT Insults used to be a highly honed art, and still should be; people are rarely more clever than when they're sharpening their fangs and nails.

A SMATTERING OF FAMOUS INSULTS:

- • • **LADY ASTOR *to* WINSTON CHURCHILL:** "If I were married to you, I'd put poison in your coffee."
- • • **WINSTON CHURCHILL *to* LADY ASTOR:** "If I were married to you, I'd drink it."

- • • **WRITER TRUMAN CAPOTE *on* WRITER JACK KEROUAC:** "That's not writing, that's typing."

- • • **WRITER GORE VIDAL *on* TRUMAN CAPOTE:** "He is a Republican housewife from Kansas with all the prejudices."

- • • **THEATER CRITIC DOROTHY PARKER *on* ACTRESS KATHARINE HEPBURN:** "She ran the entire gamut of emotions from A to B."

- • • **SOCIALITE PLAYWRIGHT CLARE BOOTHE LUCE *(holding the door open for Dorothy Parker)*:** "Age before beauty, my dear."
- • • **DOROTHY PARKER *(sailing through)*:** "Pearls before swine."

INTELLECTUALLY CURIOUS ROLE MODELS FOR WOMEN
In older Woody Allen films, the female characters took courses on existential motifs in literature or read Dostoyevsky; their heroines were Joan Didion and Gloria Steinem. Lately the cinematic role models for young women sit around endless brunches and obsess about penis size, Manolo Blahniks, and how to freeload off rich men.

INVESTMENTS It would be nice if we could revive happier versions of the word "investment"; these days, it conjures up an image of a flattened cake—or the gates of Mordor.

THE IRON FACADES OF PORTLAND In the way that America's tin ceilings inexpensively mimicked elaborate European carved ceilings, iron building fronts were evidence of great American ingenuity in adapting classical forms relatively cheaply. While countless nineteenth-century American buildings sported elaborate iron fronts, Portland's were among the most bountiful and beautiful, shaped into ornamental rows of piers, columns, and grand arches. Many of these would-be landmarks were demolished— including some of the most impressive waterfront ones, which were felled to make room for a highway—before the city became preservation-minded about them.

JACKS The beauty of this once-ubiquitous playground game is its sheer simplicity; it originated hundreds of years ago, when boys and girls played a version of the game with small stones and animal bones. Perhaps children can live without today's overly stuffed, plastic-toy-filled recreation rooms after all.

JAWBREAKERS Candy tinged with danger: What could be more enticing to a kid?

JEWELED STOMACHERS Necklaces have gotten so enormous lately— we're *almost* there. Let's just bring back the real deal. Worn by both sexes in the fifteenth and sixteenth centuries, stomachers were decorated triangular panels covering the front of a bodice; jewel-and-pearl encrusted stomachers were later worn as the showpieces of the gown ensembles by women in Europe and North America.

THE JITTERBUG Forget about spinning classes: Jitterbugging looks like it burns about ten thousand calories an hour. This vigorous swing dance was popularized in 1935 by band leader Cab Calloway, with the release of his song "Call of the Jitterbug" and the film *Cab Calloway's Jitterbug Party*. In the 1920s, the word "jitters" meant the tremors that came along with the drinking of too much bootlegged hooch; the name "jitterbug" may have come from the dance's jerky body movements.

Next time you're bored at work, go online and look up a satirical instructional short film on the jitterbug called *Groovie Movie*, made by Metro-Goldwyn-Mayer in 1944; just make sure you wear headphones.

JODHPURS The original ones that fit tightly around the calves and balloon around the thighs; these opinionated equestrian pants are best accessorized with a gin and tonic.

JOURNALISM As a seasoned editor recently told me, "When I went to journalism school, it was about, 'Afflict the comfortable and comfort the afflicted.' You wanted to keep the government honest. Today the goals are different. It's mostly about self-expression." While Facebook, Twitter, and sites of this ilk might play an increasingly important role in disseminating information, there is no replacement for the procuring of cold, hard facts in a professional manner.

As they used to say in old-guard newsrooms, "If your mother tells you she loves you, check it out."

JUKEBOXES These *objets d'art* were archaic even before the dominion of restaurant iPod playlists. The tableside jukeboxes were especially wonderful—very truck-stop chic. The Motown-playing jukebox at Ben's Chili Bowl in Washington, D.C., is almost as big a draw as the diner's 3 A.M. chili dogs, half-smokes, and cheese fries.

JULEPS These old-fashioned Southern mint and bourbon concoctions *must* be served in silver julep cups; otherwise there's no point. There are many hallowed recipes for juleps, but here is a fairly standard one: muddle four to five mint or spearmint sprigs, a teaspoon of powdered sugar, and two teaspoons of water in a julep cup. Fill the glass with crushed ice and add three ounces of bourbon. Top with more ice and garnish with a mint sprig. *Voilà!* You'll have the spins in no time.

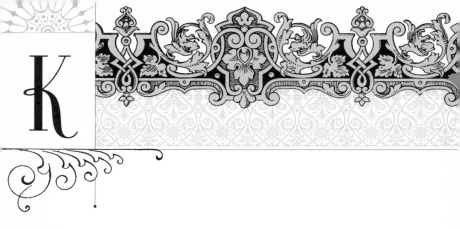

K

KAUFMAN, GEORGE (1889–1961) One of the most brilliantly acerbic playwrights of the twentieth century. Kaufman films *zing* by so quickly that I often go back and read the scripts and screenplays to savor each vicious witticism for more than a few scintillating seconds.

The owner of a famously impressive hedge of hair, Kaufman was perhaps most renowned for creating "Sheridan Whiteside," the main character of *The Man Who Came to Dinner*—whose brilliant, charismatic, preposterous *awfulness* puts him in the same hallowed club as brilliant fictional reprobates Max Bialystock, Anthony Blanche, and Royal Tenenbaum.

"KERFUFFLE" An amusingly prim, old-fashioned word for "commotion"; particularly amusing if the kerfuffle in question is not particularly prim. Two delightful but equally underused synonyms: "hoo-ha" and "hullabaloo."

KEWPIE DOLLS A phrase once used to describe particularly sweet and pretty young ladies: "Aren't you a couple of Kewpie dolls?"

The first Kewpie dolls were produced in 1913, based on artist Rose O'Neill's Kewpie illustrations from Ladies' Home Journal. Ms. O'Neill rather painfully extracted the word "kewpie" out of the word "cupid," under the premise that her creations "look like little cupids."

This term is best used ironically, in application to wretchedly behaved, filthy little girls.

"THE KINDNESS OF STRANGERS" These famous last words, uttered by Blanche DuBois—the protagonist of Tennessee Williams's play "A Streetcar Named Desire"—before she gets hauled off to the nuthouse, have brought pangs to the hearts of audience-goers for more than six decades. Because we all know that, for the most part, strangers are not kind, and, with the rise of anonymous Internet vitriol and the general deterioration of manners, they seem to get less kindly every day. Let Blanche's swan song be a lesson to us: we might all end up one day at the mercy of strangers, so let's reinstate a little kindness toward each other.

KIPPERS These little fish used to be synonymous with traditional English breakfasts; now they seem to have gone the way of English teatime. Not that you'd necessarily want to eat kippers if they were set down in front of you in the morning, but I do like the playful sound of them.

KITTEN HEELS If you can't bear the tyranny of three-inch stilettos, and you're not ready to resign yourself to the squatting effect of flats, wear kitten heels—if you can find them on today's store shelves, that is. The heels on these shoes are usually around an inch high; in the 1950s, they were sometimes referred to as "trainer heels" for young teenage girls not yet old enough to wear proper high heels. However, once Audrey Hepburn began wearing them in her '60s films, kitten heels became all the rage for women of every age.

"KNAVE" This word goes along with the following synonyms:

> cad
> scamp
> scoundrel
> heel
> rogue

In fact, there seems to be no end to the number of amusing English terms that describe a rascally man of ill-repute, especially where women are concerned.

L

LA DOLCE VITA The epitome of glamour.

Actress Anita Ekberg's midmovie jaunt through the Trevi Fountain in this Fellini film should be screened in school health classes, proving to future generations of young women that ample proportions are far sexier than today's fashionable emaciation.

LACE Lace gloves can be gorgeous. Not the hooker-y fingerless variety, but rather the coarse, crocheted kind—especially when made into driving gloves.

LADDER CHAIRS Said to have been designed by Benjamin Franklin, these chairs convert into a set of steps and back again. Popular in nineteenth-century libraries, they also became a mainstay of mid-twentieth-century kitchens. Both of my grandmothers had red metal ones in theirs; I bet yours did too.

See also MECHANICAL DESKS

LADYFINGERS The name of these old-fashioned finger-shaped sponge cake cookies managed to be dainty and vaguely ghoulish at the same time.

LADIES' CLUBS In the spirit of New York City's Colony Club. These need not be polite affairs, they just need to provide an effective community. As one enlightened businesswoman recently told me: "In the '80s, women were learning to compete with men, and now we know what they have known for centuries—you need to club together to get things done."

LADIES OF LETTERS

Oh, for a return to the lost art of letter writing. The e-mail has its place, as indeed does a text—or even a tweet—but nothing, absolutely nothing beats a thick, creamy two pages of Crane paper, smothered with news and views, lovingly folded into a tissue-lined envelope. Letters bring a voice to life, recalling memories too precious to forget.

Letters have both a personal and professional poignancy for me as a biographer. I could never have written the twin biography of Helena Rubinstein and Elizabeth Arden if relatives hadn't gifted me their scintillating letters, along with permission to print them. There is a deliciously toxic tone in a lot of their correspondence—Rubinstein's scrawled over pages of free hotel paper in her loopy handwriting, Arden's typed by her two—presumably exhausted—personal secretaries, working in eight-hour shifts from morning to midnight, spewing out orders to her staff around the world.

Fabled Hearst editor Arthur Brisbane said in 1911, "Use a picture. It's worth a thousand words." Maybe so. But no picture can take you inside the character of your subject as much as reading their letters. So let's bring back the well-dressed desk— complete with blotter, pen, and antique crystal inkwell.

—*Lindy Woodhead* • AUTHOR, *WAR PAINT: MADAME HELENA RUBINSTEIN AND MISS ELIZABETH ARDEN, THEIR LIVES, THEIR TIMES, THEIR RIVALRY*

LADY'S MAIDS In movies, lady's maids are always an invaluable source of gossip and advice, and you never have to book them in advance for a luncheon date.

THE LANGUAGE OF FLOWERS Victorians ascribed meanings to a vast array of flowers; they became a way of speaking without using words. Ladies also communicated messages by how they *wore* their received flowers: According to one scholar of Victorian flora, wearing a flower close to one's heart meant true love; a flower worn at the waist indicated interest but not commitment; and a bloom placed in one's hair was supposedly a rejection of affection.

A SHORT LIST OF TODAY'S COMMONLY AVAILABLE FLOWERS
AND THEIR VICTORIAN MEANINGS:

Amaryllis = *pride, haughtiness*

Carnation = *disdain*

Crocus = *youth*

Hyacinth = *constancy*

Jasmine = *amiability*

Lavender = *distrust*

Lilac = *first love*

Lily of the Valley = *modesty*

Peony = *anger*

Rose, red = *beauty and love*

Rose, white = *not looking for love*

Rose, yellow = *jealousy*

Tulip = *declaration of love*

Violet = *modest worth*

fig. 19: I'M TALKING TO *YOU*

I love that certain flowers have such nasty connotations; it would have *thrilled* me as a kid to give a scarlet geranium ("stupidity") to someone.

The Victorians were certainly not the only ones to use the language of flowers; it is said that nineteenth-century *demimondaines,* or courtesans, carried red camellias when they had their periods and were unavailable for amorous amusements.

LAP DESKS Wood ones with ink wells and leather tops. Lie in bed in the morning and write your to-do and grocery lists on one.

LAP ROBES Often made from fur, these were used to keep your lap and legs warm on winter buggy rides—as well as in cars and trains in the days before heating. Strike an impression next time you catch the train between DC and NYC: Wear a lap robe, and tote a wicker hamper filled with champagne, pâté, and little cakes.

LARDERS These cellars kept food cool in the days before refrigeration. Modern basements are often dingy and ugly; it would be splendid to go south and find a Hobbitlike room filled with jars of homemade preserves. As former *Vogue* editor Diana Vreeland once said: "I'm big on larders. I could take my bed and put it in a larder and sleep with the cheese and the game and the meat and the good smell of butter and earth."

LATIN When I was in school, I was given the choice of learning either French or Spanish. Why not revive the teaching of Latin to children and then let them pick a "live" language later on, once they know which one will be most relevant to their lives? Having a background in this dead language makes it easier to learn any of the following major Latin-derived romance languages:

ITALIAN

FRENCH

ROMANIAN

SPANISH

PORTUGUESE

Once the international language of science and scholarship in Europe and America, Latin also greatly influenced English; therefore, a knowledge of it greatly enhances our understanding of our own *lingua franca* and gives people a serious leg up in med school and law school.

A SAMPLING OF LATIN WORDS AND PHRASES
STILL COMMONLY USED IN DAILY AMERICAN LIFE:

- • • *Alter ego* = "the second self"
- • • *Bona fide* = "in good faith" or "authentic"
- • • *Carpe diem* = "seize the day"
- • • *Caveat emptor* = "Let the buyer beware"
- • • *De facto* = "in fact, in reality" or "already existing"

TEXT CONTINUES NEXT PAGE ⟫⟶

- • • *Et cetera* = "and so forth"
- • • *Habeas corpus* = literal translation: "You shall have the body"; in practice: a legal protection against illegal imprisonment
- • • *Ipso facto* = "by the fact itself" or "by the very nature of the deed"
- • • *Magnum opus* = "one's greatest work"
- • • *Nil* = "nothing, naught, zero"
- • • *Non compos mentis* = "not of sound mind"
- • • *Non sequitur* = "it does not follow" or "a statement containing an illogical conclusion"
- • • *Per diem* = "for each day"; in practice, a daily allowance
- • • *Post mortem* = "after death"; in practice, an autopsy
- • • *Pro bono publico* = (usually shortened to *pro bono*) = "for the public good"; in practice, service without payment
- • • *Quid pro quo* = "one thing in return for another"; i.e., "you scratch my back, and I'll scratch yours"

LAUNDRY CHUTES An ingenious bit of minor, now-arcane household architecture. They *need* to stage a comeback: Lugging a heavy laundry basket up and down the stairs is so beast of burdenish. Plus, kids adore laundry chutes; they *love* to dump all sorts of things down the hatch.

LAUREL, STAN (1890–1965) AND OLIVER HARDY (1892–1957)
One wonders why the billing for this iconic comedian duo was always "Laurel and Hardy," since Hardy was the bossy one.

fig. 20: FLEETING GLORY

LAURELS Prettier than trophies; plus, the eventual wilting of laurels is a good reminder that fame can be short-lived. Onward and upward—always.

LAWN ROLLERS Victorians took their lawns *very* seriously. Grass was not only mowed constantly but smoothed over with large hand-pushed rollers several times a month, usually right after a light rain. The result: sleek grounds that resembled shimmering emerald glass.

LAWN TENNIS More of a dance than a sport. Make sure to wear whites and drink Pimm's cocktails in between every game.

LEATHER FLYING HELMETS This would also necessitate the re-emergence of the open-top plane as a popular mode of transportation—and goggles. *Very* Amelia Earhart.

L'EGGS PANTYHOSE "EGGS" L'eggs hosiery used to market pantyhose in white plastic egg-shaped containers; they were extremely pleasing, nonsensical objects—rather Dada-esque. As a kid I found all sorts of clever uses for them.

LEISURE As a concept and a practice. Americans are very bad about taking vacations, and as a result we often drown in routine. Hard work is good for us, but routine kills the pioneer spirit for which we were once known.

LETTER CARBONS A way to preserve your own genius, since you never know if your letter's recipient will be as history-minded.

LETTER OPENERS Emblems of the *film noir* era of Hollywood; silver-screen murderers *loved* to leave bloodied letter openers strewn about for fedora-wearing, tough-talking, ciggie-smoking detectives to find. It's also rather satisfying to give junk mail a good slash or two.

THE LEWIS AND CLARK CENTENNIAL LOG CABIN Built for Portland's 1905 Lewis and Clark Centennial Exposition, this forestry building was the biggest log cabin in the world. Constructed of gigantic Douglas firs and featuring front columns made from upstanding full-length tree trunks, the building had an almost disorienting feel to it: Standing in front of it, one might be reminded of the scene in *The Nutcracker* in which the Christmas tree grows and grows to a staggering height. A Coney Island entrepreneur reportedly offered heaps of money to import this Paul Bunyanesque architectural curiosity, but it remained in Portland until it burned down in the 1960s.

LIBRARIES Both public ones and personal ones in private homes: Their disappearance would represent a step backward for civilization.

[PLATE 10]

The old man and the sea

LIGHTHOUSE KEEPERS Those romantic-looking, lone-wolf, white-bearded old men, who were of course always clad in yellow slickers and smoked pipes and read Herman Melville novels by candlelight in the company of their faithful Labradors.

LIMERICKS "The Man from Nantucket" and limericks of that ilk may be insanely juvenile and often dirty, but they always make me snicker.

LIMOUSINES These days, stretch limousines evoke images of prom parties and puking frat boys out on the town; earlier models used to embody elegance. The first automobile limousine—built around 1900—was simply a car with separate compartments for the driver and rider. Later came the "stretch limousine": a longer car designed by crafty manufacturers to capitalize on the all-American idea that Bigger = Better. Suddenly every Old Hollywood star or Chicago gangster could be spotted trolling around in one of the newly minted status inventions, and gradually they replaced private railroad cars as the luxury mode of overland travel. They were hip too: Famous big bands led by Glenn Miller and Benny Goodman used them on cross-country tours.

From that point onward, evolution was not exactly kind to the limousine: The gorgeous curves of the 1940 Cadillac limo were eventually supplanted by the ugly, boxy Lincoln stretches of the '70s and '80s and more recently with the monstrous H2 Hummer stretch SUVs. Let's have a contemporary limousine bonfire and bring back the 1908 Studebaker Brothers limousine, which might be the cutest thing I've ever seen on wheels.

LITTLE BLACK BOOKS As intimate an item as underwear; arguably more telling than a diary.

LITTLE NEMO IN SLUMBERLAND A peculiar, beautifully drafted Art Nouveau serial cartoon, *Little Nemo* by Winsor McCay first appeared in 1905 in the now-defunct newspaper the *New York Herald*. In each installment, a small boy named Nemo (Latin for "nobody") is transported nightly to a surreal dream world of jungles, Beaux Arts ice palaces, pirate ships, and miniature cities. Dream psychology was still a relatively new and engrossing concept when *Little Nemo* was introduced, and classic dream imagery fills every installment: flights, falls, shape-shifting, wild beasts, and accelerated

TEXT CONTINUES NEXT PAGE ⟫→

aging. "Slumberland is a Freudian landscape . . . [of] irrational taboos and forbidden places," observed *Publishers Weekly*. Equally bizarre are some of the recurring characters, including an impish, cigar-smoking, child-size clown named Flip and the rotund Dr. Pill, who distributes brightly hued pills from his suitcase at the drop of a hat.

The series deeply influenced many of America's great cartoon artists, from Walt Disney to Maurice Sendak; the latter has called McCay "one of America's great fantasists" and has reportedly said that this strip inspired his beloved children's book *In the Night Kitchen*.

LITTLE RED SCHOOLHOUSES As Americans moved west to the Great Plains and beyond in the early nineteenth century, one-room, red clapboard schoolhouses became a common sight in rural areas. While not exactly the stuff of staggering architecture, they are cultural emblems that deserve preservation; the vast majority have disappeared already. Also wonderful and now virtually extinct: log-cabin schoolhouses.

LIVERIED FOOTMEN I don't *care* if they're more about fashion than function; I want them back for that reason specifically.

LOBSTER NEWBERG Like champagne, the appearance of Lobster Newberg at the table used to be a sign that *serious* celebrating was taking place. Believed to have been created at Delmonico's Restaurant in 1876, this dish is a dieter's nightmare but an epicurean's delight: The lobster is absolutely *drenched* in butter, cream, cognac, sherry, eggs, and cayenne pepper.

Delmonico's chef Charles Ranhofer included the following recipe for *Lobster à la Newberg* in his book *The Epicurean* (1894):

LOBSTER À LA NEWBERG

Cook six lobsters each weighing about two pounds in boiling salted water for twenty-five minutes . . . When cold detach the bodies from the tails and cut the latter into slices, put them into a sautoir, each piece lying flat, and add hot clarified butter; season with salt and fry lightly on both sides without coloring; moisten to their height with good raw cream; reduce quickly to half; and then add two or three spoonfuls of Madeira wine; boil the liquid once more only, then remove and thicken with a thickening of egg yolks and raw cream. Cook without boiling, incorporating a little cayenne and butter; then arrange the pieces in a vegetable dish and pour the sauce over.

LOCKETS These were not used simply for containing photos: Ladies also sometimes stored a snippet of their beloved's hair inside. Lockets were also used as practical carriers for essential medicines—or even poison vials. No wonder they were so popular during Victorian times, when divorce simply wasn't an option.

LONG CIGARETTE HOLDERS They're such delightfully emphatic accessories.

LONG HAIR ON WOMEN OF ADVANCED YEARS There seems to be a mandate that women must crop their hair into short, frumpola styles when they reach a certain age. I'd hate to think that this was an implicit social commentary about older women losing their femininity and sensuality, requiring them to craft themselves into sexless objects.

My grandmother had waist-length hair for her entire adult life, and even in her nineties, she still wore it up in an elegant, dignified French twist; sometimes she'd cross two long braids over the crown of her head, or wind them into a bun at the base of her neck. Nothing is more beautiful than torrents of silver or ghost-white hair; it reminds me of unicorn manes.

LONGHAND Electronic communication has caused a proliferation of irritating abbreviations of the OMG and LOL variety; more esoteric ones include BTDT ("Been there, done that"), DLTBBB ("Don't let the bed bugs bite"), EMFBI ("Excuse me for butting in"), and ITIGBS ("I think I'm going to be sick"). Not content to restrict such inanity to computer and phone screens, people have exported such abbreviations to their actual speech, along with the truncation of certain words: "obviously" becomes "obvi"; "totally" is reduced to "tots," and so on.

Let's bring back full words and phrases; these abbreviations sound quite stupid, especially because they're usually accompanied by an intonation that would have made 1980s Valley Girls cringe. We're all busy as hell but not so rushed off our feet that we can't make time to fit in an extra *syllable*, for heaven's sake.

LONG NECKS And appreciation thereof. Now an oft-ignored attribute, long necks used to be a badge of regal elegance; you could get away with murder if you had one. Marella Agnelli—wife of Fiat magnate Gianni Agnelli, half-Neapolitan princess and one of Truman Capote's "swans"— was the proud owner of one of the most celebrated long necks in twentieth-century fashion. A *Vogue* regular, Agnelli was the subject of a now-famous 1953 Avedon portrait in which she looks practically giraffelike; it's an aston-ishing effect.

THE LORELEI These gorgeous sirens used to lure sailors to their deaths with regularity; sadly, there are very few reported sightings anymore. It seems that everyone's out of a job these days.

THE "LOST GENERATION" For a generation that was supposedly ruined by the horrors of the First World War, the members of the so-called Lost Generation—a group of mostly Paris-based writers and artists includ-ing Ernest Hemingway, F. Scott Fitzgerald, Ezra Pound, Ford Maddox Ford, and John Dos Passos—managed to turn out one of the most enduring bodies of artistic work in modern times. They were also treated to some of the twentieth century's most renowned literary salons; the most poignant epoch of Paris café culture; the exhilarating then-new sound of jazz; nights of dancing the Charleston; the height of Riviera glamour; and the mutual flush of creating timeless, ground-breaking prose and art forms. If that's what it means to be "lost," sign me up.

Few artistic cliques have been more romanticized, documented, yearned for, and emulated; God knows that we're overdue for a similar period of col-lective inspiration, although the unhappy truth is that such mass creativity often follows some sort of catastrophic international conflict.

LOST SALOON ETIQUETTE AND VOCABULARY

At bars in previous eras, patrons and bartenders communicated through a universally understood bar language. Somewhere in the 1990s, it all got muddied. Some classic bar vocabulary:

A **finger** meant that you wanted a partial shot, about a finger's worth.
Neat meant that you wanted a shot straight out of the bottle and into a glass. No chilling or shaking, just neat.
Up meant that you wanted your booze shaken or stirred or chilled and strained into a cocktail glass.
The bum's rush: Being thrown out of a bar
On the arm: A free drink
Nightcap: Your last drink of the night

For martinis, the rules went like this: The sentence "I'll have a martini" meant that you wanted a gin martini with vermouth served up. If you wanted a vodka martini, or if you wanted one on the rocks or if you had a specific brand or **call** in mind, you had to ask for it. If you didn't want a particular call, you simply said, "Whatever's in the **well**." **In and out** referred to a martini in which you put ice in a mixing glass and poured dry vermouth over it and strained it out before filling the glass with gin or vodka. **Extra dry** meant no vermouth; **dry** meant a splash of Vermouth.

Certain bar etiquette has also been lost. When a patron wanted a refill, they used to set their glass in the shot rail on top of the bar; the bartender would simply see it and come down and refill the order. When a patron was leaving their place at the bar for whatever reason, they often would place their bevnap or coaster atop their glass to signal that they were coming back: all old traditions that should come back.

—*Karl Kozel* • MUCH-BELOVED, LONGTIME NEW YORK CITY BARTENDER
AND BEVERAGE SERVICE CONSULTANT

"LOUSY" And of course the word "louse." Both just sound like what they mean. When one utters, "I got a lousy deal," nothing further needs to be said. One of my favorite literary uses of the word comes courtesy of *The Catcher in the Rye*'s Holden Caulfield: "Her hands were lousy with rocks."

See also SIMPLE WEDDING RINGS

LOVE LETTERS These days we can barely be bothered to pick up our phones to whisper sweet nothings anymore, opting instead for oh-so-romantic text messaging instead. So where does that leave the love *letter*? A low priority, I'm afraid.

Love letters, tied up with a velvet or silk ribbon and kept in a special box (which should, of course, be hidden in the back of your armoire or some-place equally secretive), will be treasured by you for decades. Don't destroy the ones from love affairs that ended badly. They are a part of your personal history, and someday—when you're older and wiser and the sting has mellowed—you may want to remember it all.

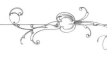

LOVE SEATS

Firstly, I love the name of it! The LOVE seat: It's where the spark happens ... there has never been a better seat designed for flirting. A glance, a touch, a whisper; an intimate conversation can be had in the middle of a party. If a girl sits there with a boy, she is really interested in him. I would still sit there with my husband!

—Coralie Charriol Paul • VICE PRESIDENT AND CREATIVE DIRECTOR, CHARRIOL INTERNATIONAL; SOCIALITE

LOY, MYRNA (1905–1993) Unlike her contemporaries Garbo and Dietrich, whose legends still shimmer, Myrna Loy—once crowned the "Queen of the Movies" by a 1936 nationwide poll of movie-goers—has unjustly faded from public memory. After transitioning out of silent films into "talkies," the golden-haired Loy became one of the film industry's most adored and highest-paid leading ladies, starring in films opposite Old Hollywood royals Clark Gable, William Powell, and Robert Montgomery. Loy worked hard to supercede the *femme fatale* roles that dominated the beginning of her career, but even in her less vampy roles, she still exuded a delicious shrewdness. Watch *Vanity Fair* (1932), in which she plays the noto-rious Becky Sharp, and you'll see what I mean.

"LUNCHEON" "Lunch" is something you grab. "Luncheon" is a civilized experience.

LUNCHTIME COCKTAILS Manhattans. Martinis. If you worked in publishing in the old days, it was mandatory to drink at least three.

LUCY AND ETHEL They showed us the farcical side of domesticity.

LUNA, DONYALE (1945–1979) Luna is considered the world's first black supermodel; 1966 was "The Luna Year," according to *Time* magazine—and yet these days her name is obscure. Born in Detroit, the 6'2" Luna moved to New York and became the first black model to appear on a cover of *Vogue*; famed fashion photographer Richard Avedon also reportedly put her under exclusive contract for a period during the early years of her career. "A creature of contrasts," read her 1966 *Time* profile. "One minute sophisticated, the next faunlike, now exotic and faraway, now a gamine from around the corner."

As if conquering the fashion world wasn't enough, Luna also appeared in Warhol films (including a 1967 film in which the model starred as Snow White) and Federico Fellini's *Fellini Satyricon.* She might have enjoyed an Imanlike reign for decades, but she died at the age of thirty-four from a drug overdose.

LUXURIOUS LUXURY GOODS Louis Vuitton (1821–1892) would likely have been horrified to see the quality of the ubiquitous goods bearing his name today. As journalist Dana Thomas aptly summarized in her book *Deluxe: How Luxury Lost Its Luster*, concerned mainly with tapping into the middle market, the luxury industry "has sacrificed its integrity, undermined its products, tarnished its history, and hoodwinked its customers. In order to make luxury 'accessible,' tycoons have stripped away all that has made it special."

Luxury used to be premised on extreme quality and—above all—rareness. If you can buy something in an airport duty-free lounge, it likely doesn't fit into this category.

m

MACGRAW, ALI (B. 1938) This 1960s and '70s silver screen icon had a wonderfully innovative approach to dressing. As her ex-husband, producer Robert Evans, recalled in his memoir, *The Kid Stays in the Picture*:

> Her entire wardrobe consisted of scarves to use as turbans, embroidered tablecloths used for wraparound skirts, etc.—naturally, all second-, third-, and fourthhand. Yet . . . each year she was on the best dressed list. Style, unlike fashion, cannot be bought nor taught. You either have it or you don't.

"MADCAP" A now-underused word meaning "wildly or heedlessly impulsive; reckless; rash"; often used in conjunction with *follies* or *antics*.

Also delightful: the related word *hijinks*: "Playful, often noisy and rowdy activity, usually involving mischievous pranks."

MAHOGANY TELEPHONE BOOTHS IN HOTEL LOBBIES
They carried a surreptitious allure; it was practically mandatory to look around furtively when you were making a call inside.

MAID'S BELLS IN DINING ROOM FLOORS An old-fashioned and now extinct household feature, maid's bells were drilled into the floor under the dining room table, so a hostess could summon the servants with a tap of her foot. These bells should *certainly* stage a comeback; even if you don't have a maid, you can use the bell to get your guests' attention, or to express your enthusiasm about a topic being discussed by dinging away.

MAIDS' STAIRCASES These back-of-house staircases, once used by servants, are a delight to come across in old houses; the stairs always creak and the stairwells are usually haunted.

MALTEDS Along with egg creams, these powder-based milkshakes were very popular at 1950s soda fountains, where they were invariably served with two straws for sharing. The following easy recipe was adapted from the "Original Old Fashioned Malted Chocolate" recipe, available at Woolworth's soda fountains in that era.

CHOCOLATE MALTED

1½ ounces chocolate syrup
3 scoops vanilla ice cream
5½ ounces cold milk
1 heaping tablespoon malted milk powder

Place all ingredients in blender and blend until smooth; pour into a chilled tall glass and top with whipped cream. Serve with two straws.

MANICURES FOR MEN This used to be a standard grooming ritual for men of quality; somewhere along the line, manicures acquired girly connotations. The unfortunate result: The modern man is forced to suffer overgrown cuticles and ratty hangnails.

MAPS They are transportable works of art; foldable adventures; infinite possibility on paper. While on the road, I love sitting in the front seat with a map on my lap and looking for amusing town names. My favorite so far: *Hot Coffee, Mississippi*.

Regarding GPS: It's annoying to be told where to go and what to do all the time. It's like being at work or school, all of that bossing around everywhere you go. Conversely, it can be a pleasure to get lost and then "find" yourself.

MARBLE BUSTS Have one made of your husband or wife: It's certainly a unique milestone birthday gift.

A decadent alternative: Have your paramour's likeness chiseled into an ice sculpture. Not very long-lasting, but then again, neither are we.

fig. 21: EMBRACEABLE YOU

MARQUISE DIAMONDS According to most sources, the marquise cut emerged in the eighteenth century, when Louis XV asked jewelers to design a diamond shape that mimicked the sultry shape of the mouth of his mistress, the Marquise de Pompadour. This shape of marquise diamond indeed resembles lips: slender and elongated with pointed ends.

Today they're largely out of style, but no one seems to know why. They actually make great stones for engagement rings: The marquise diamond's length "tricks" the eye into thinking the stone is bigger than it really is, carat-wise; you would think that today's diamond-hungry brides-to-be (and their empty-walleted grooms) would have wised up to this fact. Plus, the tapered shape flatters even the fattest finger.

THE MARX BROTHERS These boys were as madcap off camera as they were on the silver screen. Here's proof: One day MGM's Irving Thalberg—then the most powerful and feared studio producer in Hollywood—called the Marx Brothers in for a meeting; he then kept them waiting for several hours in his office while he took other meetings on the studio lot. When Thalberg finally marched back into his office, he opened the door to find the brothers sitting there buck naked, roasting potatoes on sticks in the office fireplace.

THE FIVE FAMOUS MARX BROTHERS:

1. Julius Henry "Groucho" Marx
2. Leonard "Chico" Marx
3. Adolph "Harpo" Marx (he later changed his first name to "Arthur")
4. Herbert "Zeppo" Marx
5. Milton "Gummo" Marx

A sixth Marx Brother, firstborn Manfred, sadly died in infancy.

MARZIPAN FRUIT No one seems to like the way this almond-paste candy tastes anymore, but I would wear it as jewelry, it's so pretty. A luscious piece of fruit on each finger.

"MASHER" The dictionary definition of this word is almost as amusing as the word itself:

> **mash·er** \ 'ma-shər \ *n* slang : a man who makes advances, esp. to women he does not know, with a view to physical intimacy. *Related words*: skirt chaser, wolf, woman chaser

Or, as one British etymologist puts it, "a man who thought himself irresistible to the female sex but whose advances were often unwelcome."

The word may have gone, but the need for it has clearly not.

MASQUERADE BALLS In which people actually *wear* masks. At a recent *Ballo in Maschera* given by the illustrious Young Fellows of the Frick Collection in New York City, most of the attendees showed up barefaced, lest the attending society photographers fail to identify them in pictures the next day.

Many cite Truman Capote's 1966 Black and White Ball at the Plaza Hotel as the last great American masquerade; four decades later, the fête is *still* being covered by the press, a sign of a damn good party. But even at this celebrated soiree, many guests ditched their masks as soon as possible, especially the men. "It itches and I can't see," Alfred Vanderbilt reportedly complained about his cat mask; writer George Plimpton also chucked his, claiming that it was giving off fumes. Andy Warhol—always too cool for school—didn't even bother to wear one in the first place.

MAYONNAISE

Like bread, mayonnaise has been in unfortunate exile in recent years: banished from salads, sandwiches, even coleslaw. But mayonnaise should be thought of like a fattened Christmas goose: unctuous, rich, decadent, and comforting all at once.

The best mayonnaise is most certainly homemade and barely even resembles that which comes in a jar. It is meant to be yellow, fragrant, and actually rather light.

MAYONNAISE

2 egg yolks
1 teaspoon mustard
1 teaspoon lemon juice
1 cup olive oil
Pinch of salt
1 tablespoon boiling water

All ingredients should be at room temperature. In a deep bowl, beat the yolks for 2-3 minutes until stiffened and shiny. Add the mustard, lemon juice, and salt and whisk for about 30 seconds more until everything is properly mixed together. Whisking constantly, add the oil drop by drop until it is fully incorporated and the sauce is thickened, fluffy, and stable. Finally, to prevent curdling, stir in the boiling water.

Best when served slathered on toasted country bread topped with smoked bacon and a salted slice of tomato.

— *Jennifer Lynn Leßka* • CHEF; FOOD WRITER; PROPRIETOR, FRENCH GREY RESTAURANT, NEW YORK CITY

MECHANICAL DESKS More whimsical than they sound, eighteenth-century mechanical desks were feats of design and engineering. Marie Antoinette adored them and commissioned heaps of such furniture from master cabinetmaker Jean-Henri Riesener. Each desk had all sorts of hidden compartments and secrets, and, by pressing a button, could be automatically changed from a writing desk to something else. One surviving desk, which lives at the Metropolitan Museum of Art in New York City, can be used for dining, reading, writing, or as a dressing table; buttons along the front edge of the table release lids of six hidden compartments for toiletries or writing equipment.

Investing in such versatile furnishings sounds shockingly practical for someone with Marie Antoinette's profligate reputation. But less ornate versions might make sense for space-conscious multitaskers today.

MESH ARMOR As an evening gown, it accentuates every curve.

See also RABANNE, PACO

MESSAGES IN BOTTLES A person who finds a corked bottle containing a message or a poem will likely never forget it; they seem heaven-sent.

MIDDIES Blouses or shirts with sailor collars — often worn as resort wear by women and children in the late nineteenth and early twentieth centuries. A hundred years later, still nothing looks cuter on little girls, especially tomboys.

MIDNIGHT BIRTHDAY SUPPERS A decadent way to usher in your next year of life: a feast thrown at the stroke of midnight. Such fêtes should be reminiscent of society doyenne Caroline Astor's extravagant Gilded Age midnight suppers, in which she lavished hundreds of night-owl guests with champagne and multiple courses following the latest masquerade in her famous ballroom.

MIDWAY GARDENS In 1913, revered architect Frank Lloyd Wright began construction on a grand-scale indoor/outdoor entertainment center in Chicago's Hyde Park. The finished product was considered one of the city's most glittering crown jewels; one architectural historian described it as "an incredible temple to pleasure, part pre-Columbian, part Cubist"; another called Midway Gardens "among the worldliest pieces of architecture ever created." This "pleasure temple" contained a beer garden, outdoor dance hall with band shell, several saloons, and a restaurant; unfortunately, its alcohol-heavy amusements made it a target for Prohibitionists, who succeeded in having Midway's liquor licenses revoked. Business languished, and this historical Wright masterpiece was torn down in 1929.

MILK BATHS They used to be considered the lavish cornerstone of the pampered lady's beauty regime. Famous alleged milk bathers include Cleopatra and Queen Elizabeth I, but perhaps the most famous milk bather of all was Anna Held, a musical performer and focus of the notorious, headline-dominating Milk Bath Affair of 1896. Flo Ziegfeld, the force behind the great Ziegfeld Follies show on Broadway, was determined to make Held into a globally recognized, bold-faced name; he leaked the "news" that she took a daily bath in fresh milk and even choreographed then-unheard-of media events at which reporters could see the milk bottles arrive at Held's suite. At one such event, journalists were allowed to behold Held in her *bain au lait*. This scandalous happening started an international milk bath fad and made the name Anna Held "as well known in this country as the name of the President," according to the *New York World*.

A tried-and-true recipe for milk baths:

MILK BATH

Add 2 to 4 cups of milk or buttermilk to a warm bath, soak for 20 minutes or so, and scrub your skin with a washcloth in soft, circular motions. When you are finished, rinse off with water and supposedly you will be as soft as a baby's bottom.

See also THE ZIEGFELD FOLLIES

MILK TOAST When you're bored to sobs of toast or muffins for breakfast, or feeling under the weather, make milk toast, a now-obscure nineteenth-century favorite. Celebrated food writer M. F. K. Fisher once called milk toast a "warm, mild, soothing thing, full of innocent strength" and "a small modern miracle of gastronomy." A basic version:

MILK TOAST

1 cup whole milk
2 slices white bread
Butter, sugar, and nutmeg

Butter the bread. Put in a heavy skillet over medium heat and toast until light to medium brown. Heat milk in a small pan on low heat. Do not boil. Put toast on plate, sprinkle well with sugar and a couple dashes of nutmeg. Pour hot milk over toast.

MILLER, LEE (1907–1977) Like heiress/activist Nancy Cunard, Lee Miller transcended a life of glamour for one of dedicated duty. Once a highly successful fashion model, she became an acclaimed war correspondent for *Vogue* during World War II. Responsible for some of the most powerful images of the war—and according to the Lee Miller Archives, "probably the only woman combat photo-journalist to cover the war in Europe"—Miller witnessed and documented the liberation of Paris, the battle for Alsace, and the horror of the Nazi concentration camps at Buchenwald and Dachau.

Miller was famously un-self-promoting, and much of her work was out of print and largely forgotten until her son researched and published a retrospective of his mother's photographs. Despite a recent resurgence of interest in her life, Miller remains an undersung heroine.

"MIND YOUR OWN BEESWAX" Meaning: "Mind your own damn business." There are several theories about the saying's origin. My favorite: In the nineteenth century, women used beeswax-based makeup on their faces to smooth the skin. If they sat too close to the hearth fire, the wax would start to melt. If a woman was caught staring at another's melting makeup, she would be told to "mind your own beeswax." True? Who knows. Amusing? Definitely.

MINTON'S This Harlem jazz club on 118th Street was the "music laboratory for bebop," according to trumpet legend Miles Davis. In the early 1940s, Thelonious Monk, Charlie Parker, and Dizzy Gillespie regularly jammed there, pioneering the then-new form and making mincemeat of *poseurs*. Davis colorfully describes Minton's in his autobiography, *Miles*:

> Minton's was *the* ass-kicker back in those days for aspiring jazz musicians . . . You went to 52nd Street to make money and be seen by white music critics and white people. But you came uptown to Minton's if you wanted to make a reputation among the musicians.

Minton's "kicked a lot of motherfuckers' asses" until it declined in the '60s and closed in 1974. A new version of the club recently opened in the space, under the name Uptown Lounge at Minton's Playhouse, but of course it's not the same thing.

See also THE CEDAR TAVERN

MIX, TOM (1880–1940) When asked to name the ultimate hero of Hollywood Westerns, most people would likely cite John Wayne or Gene Autry. Yet Tom Mix was Hollywood's first cowboy megastar, having made some three hundred (mostly silent) Westerns between 1909 and 1935; as a Richard D. Jensen biography about Mix states, the actor was "earning millions of dollars at a time when movie tickets cost pennies . . . [and was] as famous as baseball great Babe Ruth and world champion boxer Jack Dempsey."

Mix rode in the inaugural parades of *both* presidents Roosevelt: In 1905, he joined a group of fifty horsemen led by Rough Rider Seth Bullock in honor of Theodore. For Franklin Delano's big day, Warner Brothers sent a trainload of Hollywood stars, including Mix, who led a chorus of Busby Berkeley chorus girls down the street doing rope tricks on his horse as he went.

MODEL AIRPLANES The sort that you hang from the ceiling in a little boy's room; they were a fever-pitch hobby during the nation's midcentury love affair with aviation.

Have a peek at the main dining room of New York City's '21' Club; the ceiling is home to a formidable fleet of vintage model airplanes, among all sorts of toy trucks, cars, and other curiosities (including a model of the PT-109 motor torpedo boat, presented as a gift to '21' by President John F. Kennedy).

[PLATE II]

Keeping an eye on things

MODEL, LISETTE (1901–1983) This remarkable portrait photographer is often occluded by her most famous pupil, Diane Arbus. Both women grew famous for taking pictures of fringe members of society, including obese women and dwarves. Yet while Arbus's jarring depictions often teetered into the grotesque and painted her subjects as freaks, Model approached her subjects with tenderness; her images were often humorous and even joyous.

"MONKEY BLOCK" The historic Montgomery Block (a.k.a. "Monkey Block") building in downtown San Francisco can be likened to New York City's famed Algonquin hotel in that, for a period, it became the spiritual home to some of the West's most important artists and writers—including Robert Louis Stevenson, Bret Harte, Frank and Kathleen Norris, and Mark Twain (who reportedly met a fireman named Tom Sawyer at Monkey Block, thus setting the wheels of literary history turning)—likely partaking in the Pisco Punch famously dispensed by the building's Bank Exchange Saloon.

Considered an engineering marvel when erected in 1853 (it was then the largest building west of Chicago), Monkey Block was the first fireproof building in the city and miraculously survived the 1906 earthquake and subsequent inferno. Yet it could not withstand the brute force of demolition: The building was torn down to make room for a parking lot and is now the site of the Transamerica Pyramid.

MONOCLES Wearing one can make you look very opinionated, even if you have nothing to say.

MONOGRAMMING THE LININGS OF COATS If you investigate the lining of your grandmother's mink, chances are that her initials have been sewn into the coat's lining. I recently happened across a vintage lynx coat (floor length with three-quarter sleeves and a tag that proclaimed *Bergdorf Goodman on the Plaza)* in which the owner had her full signature embroidered inside. While the coat itself was quite eye-catching, it was the unusual signature that gave the piece *presence*.

MONTH NAMES FOR LITTLE GIRLS As in: April, May, and June. We've even recently been treated to a January, courtesy of *Mad Men* actress January Jones: very jaunty and in the spirit of Slim Keith (the original "California Girl" and a wit to boot).

Such names probably shouldn't be restricted to girls, as proven by the example of July Johnson, a cowboy sheriff in Larry McMurtry's Pulitzer Prize–winning novel, *Lonesome Dove*, or August Wilson, the playwright.

See also FLOWER-INSPIRED NAMES

THE MOON Our celestial satellite used to play a vital spiritual and practical role in the lives of humans, and we lovingly named and tracked its phases.

Each monthly full moon had a different name. Here is a list of full moon names often attributed to northeastern Native Americans:

••• **JANUARY:** *The Wolf Moon.* Named for the wolf packs that howled hungrily outside Indian villages amid deep midwinter snows.

••• **FEBRUARY:** *The Snow Moon.* Some tribes also referred to it as the *Hunger Moon*, since harsh weather conditions in their areas made hunting difficult.

••• **MARCH:** *The Worm Moon.* March meant the thawing of the ground, the reappearance of earthworms, and the return of the robins. This month's moon is sometimes called the *Sap Moon*, marking the time during which maple trees were tapped.

••• **APRIL:** *The Fish Moon.* Because this was the time that shad swam upstream to spawn. Also called the *Sprouting Grass Moon.*

••• **MAY:** *The Flower Moon.* Named for the abundance of blooms that make May so famous.

••• **JUNE:** *The Strawberry Moon.* The season in which strawberries were harvested; in Europe, it was apparently called the *Rose Moon.*

TEXT CONTINUES NEXT PAGE ⟫→

••• **JULY:** *The Thunder Moon.* Named for the violent summer storms that rumble over the country during this month.

••• **AUGUST:** *The Red Moon.* During this month, the moon often appears reddish through the late summer, sultry nighttime haze.

••• **SEPTEMBER** *and* **OCTOBER:** *The Harvest Moon.* Also called the *Corn Moon*, since these are the months in which this all-important grain is harvested. Two years out of three, the Harvest Moon comes in September; in the third year, it appears in October.

••• **NOVEMBER:** *The Beaver Moon.* Winter is on the way; the beavers are now building dams and actively preparing for the cold. This month's full moon is also sometimes referred to as the *Frosty Moon*.

••• **DECEMBER:** *The Long Nights Moon.* During midwinter nights, the moon hovers above the horizon for a long time, casting light on the frozen landscape below.

MORAN, GERTRUDE "GORGEOUS GUSSIE" (B. 1921) If you're occasionally scandalized by the attire of contemporary tennis professionals, you should have been at Wimbledon on June 20, 1949, when American tennis star Gertrude "Gorgeous Gussie" Moran sashayed out onto the court wearing a short tennis dress with ruffled, lace-trimmed knickers peeping out below the hem.

Liberally documented by the delighted press scrum (some courtside photographers laid on their stomachs to get the best view), the incident caused an international scandal; British Parliament even indignantly debated the panty-flash. Gorgeous Gussie reverted to wearing shorts after being accused of putting "sin and vulgarity into tennis"—but at least a certain sector of the clothing industry got a boost: For many years afterward, suddenly popular frilly knickers were regularly referred to as "Gorgeous Gussies" in the United Kingdom.

Moran has said that she threw the original scandalous knickers away long ago, but she still reportedly autographs and sells off similar-looking versions.

MORNING WEDDINGS The typical American wedding used to follow along these lines: a ceremony in the morning, followed by a wedding breakfast or luncheon at the bride's parents' house. The guest list: relatives and intimate friends. The couple would then leave for their honeymoon in the early afternoon. Compared to the expensive fanfare of today's circus-like weddings (the average American wedding reportedly costs upward of $20,000), the simplicity of this old ritual is very appealing.

Here is a suggested menu for an at-home "Small Wedding Luncheon" from the 1966 edition of *The New York Times Menu Cook Book*:

Vintage Punch
Liver Pâté with Pistachios
Curried Lobster Salad
Tomatoes and Green Beans à la Française
Finger Rolls

Strawberries al Asti
Wedding Cake
Coffee

See also NIAGARA FALLS

"MOTOR" As in, "Why don't we motor out to the countryside for a picnic?"

MOUSSES The savory ones have fallen out of fashion, except in the South, where they remain a worshipped art form. As food writer and Southerner Julia Reed says in her book *Ham Biscuits, Hostess Gowns, and Other Southern Specialties*, in the Mississippi Delta, "We congeal everything . . . Several years ago my mother had a four-day house party during which she served an almost exclusively gelatin-based menu." Ham was served with a hot mustard mousse; roast beef was sliced and stuffed with horseradish mousse.

A couple of years ago in Baton Rogue, I heard Reed speak about the first time she served such Southern fare at a cocktail party in New York City, where fashionable people are accustomed to spartan, joyless hors d'oeuvres. At first, people didn't know what to *do* with the punch bowl of luscious crab mousse Reed set down on the table; but when she looked again, it was empty, and the next day she was offered a job as a magazine food writer by a lucky editor who'd been there to sample the cuisine.

MRS. TROLLOPE'S BAZAAR Ever-so-refined Englishwoman Frances Trollope (1780–1863) materialized in Cincinnati one fine afternoon and, determined to bring high culture to American barbarians, erected a tiny, castlelike, glass-fronted "bazaar" in which to carry out her educational mission. Inside she set up a coffeehouse, a "picture gallery," and a music and dancing academy conducted in a ballroom; once the enterprise was completed, Mrs. Trollope opened for business and waited for her fortune to be made. Sadly but somewhat predictably, success eluded her; as an 1896 *New York Times* article commented, "probably she was utterly unfitted for the condition of a shopkeeper." She returned to England and exacted her revenge on Ohio's heathens by publishing a send-up titled *Domestic Manners of the Americans.*

Unfortunately, the delightful bazaar building that housed her misguided adventure was demolished long ago, perhaps by the descendants of the citizens once slighted by Mrs. Trollope.

MS. MAGAZINE Women still need it, for God's sake. We're not out of the woods yet.

MURALS In public *and* private spaces. They're beautiful on dining room walls and are especially important features to add to children's rooms; as Diana Vreeland once suggested in one of her famous *Why Don't You . . . ?* columns for *Harper's Bazaar*: "Why don't you paint a map of the world on all four walls of your boys' nursery so they won't grow up with a provincial point of view?" I rarely take issue with anything Vreeland said, but in this case I must indignantly add that little girls should get map murals too.

See also THE "GRAND TOUR"

MURPHY BEDS Especially popular in the 1920s and '30s, these wall beds pivoted down from a "closet" in the wall, and went right back up in the morning. They often lived behind ornate paneled doors, or at least glass ones with pretty curtains. Kids would likely love the beds, since they feel like "sneaky" furniture.

MURROW, EDWARD R. (1908–1965) Murrow's radio news broadcasts during World War II were followed by millions of listeners in the United States and Canada. Sometimes conducted standing on London rooftops during the German Blitz, his vivid reports brought the faraway conflict right into American living rooms — a jarring and then-new experience. Murrow later produced a series of TV news reports that helped lead to the censure of Senator Joseph McCarthy.

Called "the most distinguished and renowned figure in the history of American broadcast journalism" by the Museum of Broadcast Communications, Murrow was venerated for decades by all of the industry's subsequent greats. Yet my old bosses at *Nightline* were repeatedly perplexed by the fresh crops of eager newsroom interns who'd never heard the man's name.

THE MUSES In ancient Greece, these nymphs were considered sources of knowledge and providers of inspiration to creators of literature and art. Every artist should still have some sort of shrine to honor them; a scorned muse is likely to inflict writer's block, or worse.

A LIST OF THE NINE MUSES, THEIR AFFILIATED ARTS, AND EMBLEMS:

••• **CALLIOPE** — muse of epic poetry; carries a writing tablet

••• **CLIO** — muse of history; carries a scroll or tablet

••• **ERATO** — muse of love poetry; carries a lyre

••• **EUTERPE** — muse of music; carries a pipe instrument

TEXT CONTINUES NEXT PAGE ⟫→

- • • **MELPOMENE**—muse of tragedy; wears the tragic mask

- • • **POLYMNIA**—muse of sacred poetry; wears a long cloak or veil

- • • **TERPSICHORE**—muse of dance; carries a lyre

- • • **THALIA**—muse of comedy; wears the comic mask

- • • **URANIA**—muse of astronomy; carries a globe

MUSIC BOXES Little paper-covered ones with spinning ballerinas inside and a secret drawer in the back.

MUSICAL INSTRUMENTS PLAYED AT HOME Before phonograph players and radios introduced Americans to the concept of prepackaged music on demand, people heard live music exclusively, and often played their own music at home. Piano or harp skills were considered mandatory for ladies of breeding, who were often given singing lessons as well. At-home recitals for family and friends were among the most delightful Victorian diversions. (On that note, let's also bring back the musicale—shortened from the French phrase *soiree musicale*, or "evening musical party.")

Today many of us are given cursory childhood music lessons, which we are allowed to abandon once we become peevish, uncooperative adolescents. I personally took piano lessons until I was twelve; when I quit in a fit of rebellion, my mother prophesied that someday I'd regret doing so—and she was right.

MUTTON CHOPS It's just fun to say "mutton chop." If you're a woman and order a mutton chop in a restaurant, when the food is served, it will invariably be presented to the gentleman sitting across from you.

MUTTS, COMMON Today's mutts of glory are designer hybrids, genetically engineered with a precision that would have made Dr. Frankenstein shudder. A certain starlet who lives in my building flounces around with a "Teacup Maltipoo" in tow (translation: a cotton-ball-sized Maltese crossed with a poodle). Other carefully curated canine crossbreeds include the "Gointer" (a golden retriever–English pointer mix), the "Bullador" (a Labrador–English bulldog mix), and the "Giant Schnoodle" (a giant schnauzer–standard poodle mix). The list of such permutations is seemingly endless, and more than a little bit creepy.

Yet once upon a time, the most adored dog in America was a common mutt: Little Orphan Annie's Sandy, a comic-book dog of decidedly random lineage. "[Sandy] is often referred to as an Airedale; but, in truth he was part Airedale, part collie and, perhaps, part something else," announced *Dog & Kennel* magazine after careful deliberation. The dog who played Sandy for the entire run of the Broadway musical Annie was also an abused rescue mutt in real life; his owner bought him for $8 on the day the dog—a terrier mix—was scheduled to be euthanized.

Let us exalt once again the common mongrel: a humble, scrappy dog of mixed or indeterminate breed. Perhaps loyalty and love don't have to have such scientifically calculated origins.

MYSTERY In previous generations, women didn't let men see them shave their legs; a curated manner of presentation was important to them. Today's show-and-tell-all culture encourages the parading of even the most intimate and mundane details of one's life in public. A cultivated mystery is at the root of allure—just ask Dietrich and Garbo. Both sexes should remember to leave *some* things to the imagination.

n

"NAIL LACQUER" Because what we call "nail polish" today is not polish. It is a lacquer.

NAPS Taking a short afternoon nap used to be considered good common sense. These days, naps seem to be regarded as indulgences on par with buying a floor-length mink coat. Whenever I feel guilty about taking a nap, I remember what Augustus McCrae said in *Lonesome Dove*: "I'm glad I ain't scared to be lazy." In this context, a nap becomes an act of bravery, which makes it okay.

NEAPOLITAN ICE CREAM Strawberry, vanilla, and chocolate side by side: This combination of pink, white, and brown should be made into the flag of some languorous, pleasure-oriented country. Most popular in the late 1800s—before freezers were common—Neapolitan ice cream was considered an extravagant treat. It's still a gorgeous sight when presented as a block on a glistening silver platter, served as cut slices.

NECESSAIRES In centuries past, travelers often brought their own silverware and toilette accessories with them, since getting around took so long and you never knew what you'd find on the road (or at your destination, for that matter). Lowly travelers trotted around with a passel of knives and forks, but fancier creatures toted beautiful cases called *necessaires*, filled with everything from gold scissors to full sets of silver cutlery to writing utensils to crystal brandy carafes. This seems terribly sensible to me: There's nothing more off-putting than getting dirty silverware in a restaurant.

NECK SCARVES There was a time when "a scarf [was] to a woman what a necktie [was] to a man," as Christian Dior put it. To the modern eye, a neck scarf can look sock hop-ish, but perhaps it's time to retrain our aesthetics on this count. Prettily tied little silk scarves are a lovely way to infuse an outfit with flair and a punch of color—and are an inexpensive way to accessorize.

If you're an aficionado of the longer variety of neck scarves, do take care to avoid an Isadora Duncan–style fate: The dancer was well-known for her love of dramatic, billowing scarves; one ill-fated day in 1927, as she drove about in an open-topped car, her hand-painted silk scarf fluttered out a *little* too far and became entangled around one of the car's rear wheels.

And that was the end of Isadora Duncan.

NEEDLEPOINT BELTS

From junior high through high school I would needlepoint belts for myself or as gifts for my friends. I would personalize them with monograms, stripes, lobsters, etc. My favorite is one that my husband still wears that has fly-fishing hooks all over it. Too great!

—Kate Spade • DESIGNER

NEW ORLEANS On par with the other beautiful water-based cities of our world, New Orleans is one of America's great national treasures—and should be treated as such. Italy would never let Venice "sink" and disappear; the Netherlands would never surrender the canal city of Amsterdam to the gods of weather (or the dunce gods of bureaucratic incompetence). The city is still trying to get its land legs after Hurricane Katrina nearly turned it into a modern Atlantis, and it still faces such a fate if we don't protect it properly.

NEW YEAR'S DAY PARTIES These days, the New Year is usually commemorated with New Year's Eve parties (often disappointing, overly hyped affairs at best, and wretch-fests at worst). It would be nice to spend New Year's Day happily anticipating the future, not nursing a hideous hangover and making penitent, unrealistic resolutions.

This year, why not set the tone for the year ahead by inviting your most adored friends to an old-fashioned New Year's Day buffet lunch or dinner? The Victorians were crazy about them, and Southerners still are, serving collard greens (a symbol of money) and "lucky" black-eyed peas. There are also interesting superstitions about what *not* to serve at a New Year's Day party: lobster, for example, "because they move backward and could therefore lead to setbacks," according to the food Web site Epicurious. "Chicken is also discouraged because the bird scratches backward, which could cause regret or dwelling on the past," it warns. Apparently you're also supposed to avoid "eating any winged fowl, because good luck could fly away."

NEWSPAPERS A seriously endangered species. They fall into the "don't know what you've got until it's gone" category.

NIAGARA FALLS Especially as a honeymoon locale.

Niagara Falls used to be equally famous as a destination for daredevils. One of the most astonishing stunts was undertaken in 1901 by sixty-three-year-old Michigan schoolteacher Annie Edson Taylor; some sources call her the first person to survive a trip in a barrel over the Falls. A tad battered and bloodied after plunging down Niagara's Canadian Horseshoe Falls, Taylor scraped herself out of the barrel and reportedly said, "Nobody ought ever do that again."

NIGHTCAPS With tassels, of course.

NIGHTTIME Apparently, if we don't watch out, nighttime is going to go the way of the dinosaurs. Not because the world will stop turning on its axis, but because of what *National Geographic* recently called "light pollution." Our world is becoming bathed in ubiquitous artificial light, emptying city skies of stars.

1950s GIRDLES AND BRASSIERES

A 1950s brassiere is like a beautifully designed suspension bridge. They are so Azzedine Alaïa, if you know what I mean. When I was a kid even skinny women wore fabulous long-line girdles. They can give you the most extraordinary shape and the tiniest waist. If a girdle is too uncomfortable, then maybe try a structured Frederick's of Hollywood cone-shaped brassiere. Black! I hope this suggestion does not make me sound like a kinky pervert. I just think the designs are so exquisite.

—*Simon Doonan* • CREATIVE DIRECTOR, BARNEYS NEW YORK;
AUTHOR, *ECCENTRIC GLAMOUR*

[PLATE 12]

away we go

1950S SCI-FI B MOVIES In the '50s, there was a huge uptick in the number of sci-fi and space movies made in America; some of the more prominent films included *The War of the Worlds* (1953), *Invasion of the Body Snatchers* (1956), and *The Day the Earth Stood Still* (1951). As science fiction novelist J. G. Ballard once stated, "People, by the fifties, had lost their optimistic confidence in the ability of science to fulfill all the dreams of mankind; instead, you saw science about to fulfill all the nightmares of mankind."

All this anxiety aside, the special effects in some of these films are hilarious. A favorite in our household was *The Killer Shrews* (1959), in which a gaggle of witless people are trapped on an island with a scientist whose experiments have somehow created giant man-eating, island-dwelling shrews. Shots of these menacing beasts consist of yard dogs with pelts strapped to their backs leaping up and down at a wooden fence.

SOME OF THE MORE AMUSINGLY NAMED TITLES:

Attack of the Crab Monsters (1957)
The Brain Eaters (1958)
Devil Girl from Mars (1954)
The Incredibly Strange Creatures Who Stopped Living and Became Mixed-Up Zombies (1964)
It Came from Beneath the Sea (1955)
It Came from Outer Space (1953)
It Conquered the World (1956)
Night of the Blood Beast (1958)
Radar Men from the Moon (1952)
Robot Monster (1953)
Them! (1954)

NINTENDO I mean the original 1985 NES console, with games like *Super Mario Bros. 2, The Legend of Zelda, Hogan's Alley, Duck Hunt, Mike Tyson's Punch Out!!,* and *Adventure Island,* among others; as a kid, I could also get sucked into *The Goonies II* for hours. While exceedingly remedial by today's standards, they're a refreshing change from video games featuring hookers and drive-by shootings.

NIXIE CLOCKS A 1950s innovation as difficult to unearth as black truffles, the nixie clock's "face" consisted of small bell jar–shaped valves containing neon digits depicting the time. So many "futuristic" objects from that era now look laughably dated; the nixie clock, however, still looks startling and modern.

NOSEGAYS They probably should have found a nicer word than "nosegay" for these traditional small bunches of sweet-smelling flowers; sometimes the words "posey" or "tussie-mussie" were substituted. Originally toted around by ladies in medieval times, nosegays were worn around the neck to help mask unpleasant street smells, of which there were *many*. The bouquet's job was literally to keep the nose "gay"—hence its unfortunate name.

Later nosegays rose to popularity as a Victorian fashion accessory. Typically, nosegays were gifts to ladies from suitors. The bouquets were often attached to the woman's hip—or nestled at her flushed bosom—and the types of flowers used carried all sorts of messages.

I love the idea of wearing flowers that you are given as a gift: except, of course, when you hate the flowers. It's nice to have the option but not the obligation.

NOSES Interesting ones that lend a face character. Today nose jobs are given as "Sweet Sixteen" presents; soon they'll be doled out at Communion or even baptisms. I've heard that no plastic surgeon would ever touch Barbra Streisand's amazing nose for fear of ruining her voice. A few other glamorous owners of singular noses include Cleopatra, Caesar, poet Anna Akhmatova, Diana Vreeland, actors Owen Wilson, Meryl Streep, Sarah Jessica Parker, Rosemarie DeWitt, and Anjelica Huston (who once reportedly said, "There were times when I hated my nose. But you grow up and you start to recognize that maybe it wasn't a bad thing that you weren't born Barbie").

"NOTHING TO WRITE HOME ABOUT" Such a grandmotherly turn of phrase, yet *so* withering.

NOTIONS DEPARTMENTS I adore the idea of going out to shop for one's notions. Yet actual notions departments peddled not ideas and opinions, but rather all sorts of sewing supplies: thread, patterns, ribbons, buttons—the works. They used to be mainstay features of major department stores in bygone eras, when ladies still sewed much of their own wardrobes.

As kids, my best friend and I used to run like wild animals into the notions department at Hahne's and tear into bags of brightly colored feathers: a thousand times more gratifying than a pillow fight.

NUNNERIES As in "get thee to a nunnery." A more fitting destination for some of today's beastly little starlets, who treat rehab as a photo op. Those mean old nuns would make sure those girls wore underpants in front of the paparazzi.

O

OAK ALLEYS Often planted in the antebellum South, these parallel, symmetrical live tree rows provided spectacular entranceways to mansions. One of the most famous surviving oak alleys adorns the historical Louisiana plantation house Bon Sejour (which, thanks to the trees, is referred to almost exclusively as "Oak Alley"); the centuries-old oaks there are as heavy as the Louisiana summer air. The bottom branches are so lazy that they lie across the lawns instead of reaching up into the sky.

Local lore tells of a fantastical 1850 wedding that took place on a Louisiana oak-flanked road known as "The Incredible Avenue." A nearby plantation owner had his servants release large spiders into the trees several days before the festivities; the spiders wove great webs throughout all the branches. On the morning of the wedding, the servants blew gold and silver dust from fireplace bellows into the alley, turning the webs into shimmering, billowing metallic canopies. The wedding procession was then led down this ethereal, iridescent corridor.

OFFERING CANDLES IN CHURCHES In some much-visited churches and cathedrals, wax offering candles are being replaced with electronic ones. Little more than grids with bulbs, these machines are coin operated: You plunk in a quarter and this dumb little orange light comes on somewhere on the grid. It's a dinky, soulless effect.

See also GRAVESTONES

OLD FARMER'S ALMANAC First published in 1792, the *Old Farmer's Almanac* is North America's oldest continuously published periodical; it used to play a central role in the lives of Americans, especially in rural areas. This periodical is most famous for its uncannily accurate long-range weather predictions: It has traditionally boasted an 80 percent accuracy rate for forecasts made up to two years in advance. The *Almanac*'s publishers are highly secretive about the methods they use to make their predictions, stating cryptically that the founding editor's formula relied on "a complex series of natural cycles." Today that formula is supposedly "kept safely tucked away in a black tin box at the *Almanac* offices in Dublin, New Hampshire." The *Almanac*, whose mantra is "Useful, with a pleasant degree of humor," also includes information such as moon calendars, sunrise and sunset data, birthday lore, and everyday advice in the form of money-saving tips and recipes for natural remedies.

In recent years, as our modern lives have become increasingly divorced from the cycles of nature, the *Almanac* has acquired the patina of a sentimental curiosity. Yet its charmingly hokey content—if you can *find* it amid the ads for lawn mowers, bush trimmers, and even cell phones—should feel more relevant than ever: After all, the publication's centuries-old core values (conservation, sustainable living, and simplicity) have become rather trendy in recent years.

OLD-FASHIONED ICE BAGS The sort that grandmothers and cartoon characters would put on their heads to cure headaches. They also brought humor to the soothing of hangovers.

ONE-PIECE SWIMSUITS Bikinis are grand, but it's hard to live up to their expectations.

OPERA Still sacred to many, but losing ground with each passing year to more modern diversions. In eras past, even small towns often sported clapboard opera houses; by comparison, even today's regal metropolitan ones are struggling to make ends meet.

OPERA CAPES In velvet: You become as dramatic as the opera taking place on stage.

OPERA GLASSES These are equally useful—and make quite an impression—at boxing matches and other such sporting events.

ORACLES These would be especially helpful on lottery-drawing days, when the kitty is absolutely overflowing.

ORGAN GRINDERS Just so we can see the monkeys in those cute little vests and fezzes again.

ORNAMENTAL LILY AND GOLDFISH PONDS Like having a live Matisse painting in your backyard.

ORNATE CEILINGS Ceilings used to sport all sorts of carvings, elaborate plaster work, murals and paintings, exposed beams, and so on. In today's architecture and interior design, ceilings are often a forgotten surface and are left plain as pudding.

[PLATE 13]

a little monkey business

OUTDOOR CHILDHOODS

In the summer of 1947, Spencer Cowan and I were best friends, and Haslemere Gardens, just off North Circular Road on the outskirts of London, was our turf. I believe we ate lunch and supper; but I have no recollection of anything but uninterrupted daylight hours outdoors that lasted sixteen hours or more. Our activities were largely experimental: How far can you walk on the curb with your eyes closed? Answer: Until you run into a lamppost and break your nose. How does one make lavender water? Answer: We still don't know for sure, but it requires something more than marinating lavender in water. How do you contain a small fire in a large, dry field? Answer: You don't. (I am assuming that the statute of limitations for arson in Great Britain is less than sixty years, and anyway, to the best of my knowledge, no one died.)

We caught tadpoles, reenacted Robin Hood's epic fight with Little John using our hand-cut staves, and spent hours cutting and stripping the bark off saplings and branches, which we turned into an armory of bows and arrows.

Of all the hours during that endless summer, I remember only fifteen minutes a day in the proximity of an electronic device. We listened on the radio to the adventures of *Dick Barton, Special Agent*, who, with his faithful companions, Snowy and Jock, provided the inspiration for some of our activities the next day. Although, to be perfectly frank, I don't believe that Agent Barton ever tried to make lavender water— even for his mother.

— *Ted Koppel* • JOURNALIST; COMMENTATOR; LONGTIME ANCHOR, ABC NEWS

OVERDOORS These once-popular old-fashioned ornamental panels were hung in the bare area between a door top and the ceiling. Like curtains affixed well above a window top (one of the oldest decorating tricks in the book), overdoors enhanced the feeling of height in a room and remain the next best thing to oversize doors themselves.

OVERSIZE CUTLERY In heavy silver, of course: an old grand hotel mainstay.

OVERSIZE PEARLS Preferably the size of quarters: You *never* see them anymore. Bear in mind that pearls used to be rarer and more valuable than diamonds, so you can just *imagine* the impression that the big whoppers must have made.

OVERSIZE HEART-SHAPED VALENTINE'S DAY CHOCOLATE BOXES Valentine's Day is unadulteratedly cheesy. If you're going to observe it, you might as well kitsch things up. The box should be covered in some approximation of red velvet or satin and be festooned with a delightfully tacky fake rose.

P and Q

PACIFISM For obvious reasons.

PAGODAS Especially the once-ubiquitous roadside ones that housed all-American fast food. One of the best examples: Walter's Hot Dog Stand in Mamaroneck, New York, which has resided under a copper-roofed Chinese pagoda since 1928. For more than eighty years, Walter's adoring patrons have sent postcards to the owners from all over the world; the collection includes one from President Calvin Coolidge and another from a member of Admiral Byrd's 1929 Antarctic expedition.

PAINTED PORTRAITS A vastly superior alternative to mall photos of the kids; unlike staged mall shots, someone may actually *want* these paintings later.

THE PALM BEACH SLEEPER Hardly anyone is dying to take the train from New York to Palm Beach anymore, and probably for good reason: I doubt that the current railway accommodations are up to the standards of the glamorous Palm Beach sleeper mentioned in *Auntie Mame*. I wish the old version were still around, with mahogany-walled, swinging crystal chandelier–laden dining cars and lovely sleeper berths cloaked by velvet curtains. Life is supposedly about the journey and not the destination, and there are so few modern modes of transportation that prove this saying true.

PALM COURTS A popular feature in Gilded Age hotels. The era's most famous American indoor palm court resided inside the original Waldorf-Astoria Hotel (which was razed to make way for the Empire State Building): The "Palm Garden" was enclosed in glass, to display its dining socialites and celebrities like expensive jewelry to voyeurs on the wrong side of the panes. Author H. G. Wells once wrote of the scene: "From an observant tea-table beneath the fronds of a palm, I surveyed a fine array of these plump and pretty pupils of extravagance."

Today it's hard to find an older hotel palm court that hasn't lost its luster; yet it would be lovely if someone could whip up a new batch—and make them *very* thick with palms, so you'd feel like you were in an Arabian date grove.

See also CAFÉ SOCIETY

PALM READINGS A good reminder that your destiny really *is* in your hands.

PALMER METHOD PENMANSHIP If you look at old birthday cards or letters from your grandparents, their handwriting was likely scripted in the Palmer Method, the predominant type of penmanship taught in American schools during the first half of the twentieth century. I love seeing the looping, old-fashioned *Q*s, which look like floppy 2s on vintage flea-market postcards. Palmer penmanship was both legible and ornate; today's personality-less taught script is usually neither.

PAPER DOLLS I was startled to learn of the presence of virtual paper dolls; I visited one of the most popular paper doll Web sites and learned that you can "dress" Paris Hilton (and *Perez* Hilton, for that matter) and play a "Paparazzi Game," in which you can "take a clear picture of the celebs [sic] face for a perfect score." Some people were likely horrified in the same way when Barbie dolls first came along, but the tenor of this new phenomenon seems trashy in an unprecedented way. Let's bring back *paper* paper dolls of a quainter variety; one of the best parts about playing with such dolls was cutting and pasting together your own designs for them, mimicking the actual process of making real clothing.

fig. 22: SHADE
YOUR BEAUTY

PARASOLS The difference between umbrellas and parasols: The former is for protection against rain, the latter against the sun. Used since ancient times in many cultures, parasols largely fell out of favor in the West when Victorian fashions gave way to more modern ensembles. I'm keeping my fingers crossed that some influential designer or fashion editor popularizes them again; they're such pretty practicalities.

PARKER, SUZY (1933–2003) In the 1950s, Parker became the first fashion model to earn a then-staggering $100,000 per year; she and her sister Dorian Leigh are considered by many to be the world's first supermodels, along with Lisa Fonssagrives. The flame-haired Parker graced the covers of dozens of magazines around the world. Designer Christian Dior called Parker "the most beautiful woman in the world"; Eileen Ford, doyenne of modeling agents, once said of her: "She was everybody's everything."

The sort of celebrity enjoyed by Parker and her contemporaries was a far cry from the often-bratty variety that emerged during the supermodel era of the 1980s and '90s, embodied by Linda ("We don't wake up for less than $10,000 a day") Evangelista and maid-assaulter Naomi Campbell. The old girls always maintained a sense of regal decorum; one really can't imagine Suzy Parker beaning her housekeeper in the head with a cell phone.

PARLORS Precursors to today's living rooms, parlors were used for receiving and entertaining guests, and for after-dinner family amusements. Much of the household's most impressive furnishings and works of art resided in these rooms, on display to visitors. Houses of means often had separate parlors for ladies and gentlemen. Ladies' parlors often sported musical instruments like pianos and harps, card tables, sewing and embroidery kits; ample bars and billiards tables hulked in the men's room. I see no reason for ladies not to have billiards and booze in modern versions of *their* parlors—*anything* in the name of progress.

PARLOR GAMES How Victorians spent the then-new phenomenon known as "leisure time." Most parlor games were of the self-bettering variety, often involving logic or word play; parlor diversions of this variety that are still familiar today include Brainteasers and Twenty Questions.

Some parlor games are still delightful for children's birthday parties, like charades and musical chairs; here are a few lesser-known but amusing ones for such celebrations.

LOOKABOUT

The birthday girl shows everyone a little knickknack in the room. All the guests then leave the room while she hides it. The guests then come back into the room and everyone looks for the item; when someone spots it, they are to sit down without saying a word. Advise children to continue to mill around for a few seconds before they sit down, making it more difficult for others to locate the item. The last one to find the object hides a new item for the next round.

YOU'RE NEVER FULLY DRESSED WITHOUT A SMILE

One person is selected to be "It"; he or she is the only one in the group who is allowed to smile. He or she can do anything they want to try and get the others to smile; the first one who does so then becomes "It." The last child to smile is declared the (rather stern) winner.

PASS THE SLIPPER

Players sit on the floor in a circle. One child sits in the middle; she must close her eyes while the slipper is passed from person to person behind their backs. When the center person opens her eyes, the passing immediately stops and she must guess who's holding the slipper. If the guess is correct, they trade places. If it's wrong, the kid in the center closes his or her eyes again and the passing starts again.

One particularly bizarre parlor game called SNAPDRAGON—popular from the sixteenth to the nineteenth centuries—entailed setting a wide bowl of brandy filled with raisins on fire. The goal: to pluck the raisins out and eat them without burning yourself to a crisp (one source states that you were supposed to *bob* for these raisins with your *mouth*). Probably best to leave this one off the birthday party roster.

PARMA VIOLETS An exotic branch of the violet family that gives off a beautiful, strong fragrance, parmas were often worn by Victorian ladies in a bouquet tied to the waist or pinned to the bosom. These sweet, hard-to-cultivate, exotic flowers sadly went out of fashion as both plantings and accessories after World War I.

PARTY-LEAVING ETIQUETTE

One skill that seems to have disappeared from today's roster of good behavior is knowing when and how to leave a social gathering—whether an invitation for a cup of tea, or a luncheon or dinner party at a hotel or on a houseboat, or an enormous cocktail reception on someone's roof. Guests overstay their welcome—again and again. If you're invited to "a reception from 6 to 8," for example, everyone should be in the act of leaving by 8:30. Those who linger are hurting the host's wallet (to force the catering staff into unnecessary overtime is expensive and thoughtless). If you know you are going to have to leave early, always tell your hosts in advance—preferably when you are accepting the invitation in the first place. Whether it's a dentist's appointment, or a horse race you want to watch on TV because you've bet a wad of money on it, or the funeral of your boss's father that you should attend, there are always legitimate reasons for arriving late or leaving early, provided you have properly communicated them to your hosts.

In your own home, be tough about making your friends or business associates leave. I would always jump up like a jack-in-the-box a half hour after the party was supposed to end and announce dramatically to the people sitting there, perhaps slightly soused from too many drinks, "Well, it's time for everyone to go home and get a good night's sleep. The most important people in Washington are right here, in this room tonight, and if they are not in good shape for handling the government's problems tomorrow, none of them will be solved!" It always worked. The guests felt they were indeed *that* important, and that if they drank too much tonight or got too little sleep, there would be serious repercussions tomorrow in the affairs of state!

— *Letitia Baldrige* • ETIQUETTE EXPERT, JACQUELINE KENNEDY'S
WHITE HOUSE SOCIAL SECRETARY

PATRON SAINTS Some saints get to be patrons of deeply specific demographics. Some of my favorites:

- • • **SAINT BERNARD**—patron saint of beekeepers
- • • **SAINTS COSMAS** *and* **DAMIAN**—patron saints of hairdressers
- • • **SAINT JOB**—patron saint of breeders of silkworms
- • • **SAINT JAMES THE LESS**—patron saint of hatters
- • • **ERATO** Saint Valentine—patron saint of lovers and epileptics (a curious combination)
- • • **SAINT WENCESLAUS**—patron saint of prisoners and altar boys (another curious combination)
- • • **SAINT BLAISE**—patron saint of mattressmakers

My little French bulldog sports a small collar charm bearing the image of St. Francis of Assisi, the patron saint of animals; careless people might want to invest in a charm bearing the image of St. Anthony, patron saint of lost items. In the novella *Breakfast at Tiffany's*, the narrator gives a gift to the restless, rootless, forever-on-the-move Holly Golightly: a medal with an emblem of St. Christopher, the patron saint of travelers.

PATTERNS In previous eras, if you saw a dress you liked in *Vogue* or some such, you could often buy the pattern and make the dress yourself—which is a very democratic, humane approach to high fashion. You can still buy 1950s and '60s patterns online for classic Givenchy-style dresses, gowns, jackets, and skirts; bring one to your tailor and he or she can create the garment for you for far less money than a retail version.

PEARL, CORA (1835–1886) One of England's more famous nineteenth-century exports, Pearl had the distinction of becoming the so-called Queen of Paris Courtesans; before she died, she left behind *The Memoirs of Cora Pearl: The Erotic Reminiscences of a Flamboyant 19th Century Courtesan,* which remains a must-read. In this detailed, graphic look into the world of the demimonde, Pearl dishes on the sexual prowess and predilections of her many famous lovers, who hailed from all walks of life; she also includes a scene in which she was served on a platter at a dinner party, naked and slathered in cream—surely the juiciest course.

See also COLETTE

PEGGY GUGGENHEIM'S SUNGLASSES COLLECTION
Not satisfied to have priceless works of art hanging from every wall (and stashed in the leaky basement) of her Venetian palazzo, Peggy Guggenheim *wore* art in many forms: architectural earrings by Alexander Calder, painted dresses by Elsa Schiaparelli—and perhaps most famously, gesso sunglasses by American artist Edward Melcarth. One pair resembled a large bat with its wings spread across her eyes and the creature's body comprising the bridge; another pair mimicked a Surrealist butterfly with pronged wings.

See also THE ART OF THIS CENTURY GALLERY

PENMANSHIP Like good posture, it's an indicator of elegance and individuality. It's easier than you might think to "invent" your handwriting.

PENNY ARCADES Precursors to the video arcades of the 1970s and '80s, penny arcades were amusement park venues where, for the price of a penny, you could play any one of a myriad of coin-operated entertainments. These arcades emerged in the nineteenth century and featured all sorts of love testers, pinball machines, and even peepshows (not necessarily pervy ones, but ones that showed simple short animations and such). By the '50s, such coin-operated amusements were considered corny and were replaced by sportier stalls with shooting galleries and Skee-Ball-type fare.

I'd give my eyeteeth to have one of those old penny arcade fortune teller machines; you'll likely remember "Zoltar" the fortune teller from the movie *Big*. One brand, called the Genco Gypsy Grandma, has a figure that actually appears to *breathe* inside that glass box. Her chest moves in and out, and after dispensing a fortune card to the patron, ol' Gypsy Grandma blows him a kiss and goes back to sleep. A little creepy—but you can't help believing a prophesy administered by such a creature.

PENNY LOAFERS Have good luck at your feet all day long.

[PLATE 14]

an unusual worldview

PERFUME ATOMIZERS Crystal ones with tasseled bulbs, of course. Perfume atomizers used to be considered a high form of boudoir elegance for women, and they were lovingly passed down as heirlooms to daughters and granddaughters in the way that men used to pass down their watches. They largely disappeared with the rise of mass-marketed perfumes in disposable bottles and when women stopped keeping vanity tables in their bedrooms.

"PERSNICKETY" It's very fun to say, although its contemporary synonyms are as well: "nitpicky," "fussy," and "finicky."

PERSONALIZED PERFUMES Scent is such a particular thing: What woman wants to step into an elevator and smell her perfume on some other broad? Perhaps it's time to bring back local perfumers to create trademark fragrances for us.

One of Marie Antoinette's personal perfumes was recently reproduced from notes by Versailles' former palace perfumer, Jean-Louis Fargeon—found among some centuries-old documents warehoused by the French government. The result—dubbed *Sillage de la Reine*, or "In the Wake of the Queen"—was described as an amber essence of jasmine, orange blossom, tuberose, iris, cedar, and sandalwood.

PETTICOAT MIRRORS Popular in the nineteenth century, these narrow mirrors mounted on the bottom of a parlor or dining room hall console allowed ladies to check whether their petticoats were showing. Even though we could care less today whether our petticoats are showing or not, such mirrors would give us a nice opportunity to admire our often too-expensive shoes.

PHONE CONVERSATIONS Supplanted by e-mails and texting, they're becoming as archaic as handwritten letters.

fig. 23: RING MY BELL

PHONE NUMBERS THAT INCLUDE EXCHANGE NAMES
I just love the idea of picking up the phone and telling someone, with great flourish: "Give me Victor 9, darling."

During the early years of telephone service, cities and towns with more than 10,000 phone numbers used exchange names at the beginning of their numbers. Telephone numbers used to begin with two letters, which were an abbreviation for a word.

SOME OF THE MORE FAMOUS OLD-STYLE EXCHANGE PHONE NUMBERS:

• • • The infamous BU 8 (i.e., butterfield 8)

• • • MU 5-9975 (i.e., Murray Hill 5-9975) was one of the Ricardos' phone numbers on *I Love Lucy*.

• • • The number in the Glenn Miller Orchestra's hit song **"PENNSYL-VANIA 6-5000"** was and is the number of the Hotel Pennsylvania in New York City. If you call the number, now written as (212) 736-5000, you will still reach that hotel.

PIANO SHAWLS Originally used to protect the glistening tops of Steinways and Baldwins from nicks and dirt, these shawls—often made from velvet with fringed edges, or silk with floral patterns—were later co-opted by cheeky females as evening-wear accessories. They hung as nicely on the curves of the body as they did on the curves of baby grands.

PIANOS They used to be mainstays in households of all classes.

PICNICS IN GRAVEYARDS People often used to have luncheons in graveyards, visiting the grave of a loved one or simply admiring picturesque historical cemeteries; there was nothing sinister about it. Some cookbooks even used to suggest menus for such outings:

Menu for a Picnic a Deux in a Graveyard

Double Consommé with Sherry or Manzanilla

Foie-Gras Naturel

Asparagus Vinaigrette

French Bread

Strawberry Tarts

—From *Picnic Book* by Nika Hazelton, 1969

"PICTURE" As in, "We're going to see the Bette Davis picture." Equally wonderful: "talkie."

THE ORIGINAL *PINK PANTHER* MOVIES There is only one Inspector Clouseau, and that is Peter Sellers.

PINK POODLES To many, poodles are synonymous with preening and ridiculousness; one might as well dye them pink to drive the point home. Onetime pinup girl and *Dynasty* doyenne Joan Collins was the quintessential pink poodle owner; look up the famous 1955 publicity photos of Collins reclining demurely on her pink bed with pink pillows, a pink rotary phone in the background, while caressing a *very* pink poodle.

PINK SUITS FOR MEN America's most famous pink suit likely belonged to the great Gatsby (a "gorgeous pink rag of a suit," to be exact)—but these garments should certainly not be relegated to the pages of fiction *or* the 1920s. While many men today dismiss them as effeminate, they can also be the ultimate badge of manliness: As in, you're so comfortable in your own skin that you'll wear one without giving a damn what anybody else thinks.

PIPES So few men smoke them anymore. People either really love or really despise the smell of pipe tobacco; to me, it has always represented the feeling of deep satisfaction. Maybe that's because it was the sort of thing done at the end of the day, after dinner, with a full belly and a book on your lap.

PLANS Make them, keep them, show up on time. The advent of mobile communication has made people habitually tardy and unreliable. Just because you text someone a thousand times telling them that you're going to be late—or not make it at all—doesn't excuse the fact. This entry is also an act of self-admonishment; I am guilty as hell of this offense.

THE PLAZA HOTEL The hallowed New York City home of children's book heroine Eloise, the Plaza recently underwent an overhaul that converted most of the guest rooms into private condos, dismaying history-minded visitors. An incongruously modern, neon-lit bar now resides in the new lobby; the once-iconic Palm Court is stuffed with drearily modern upholstery; the atmospheric Oyster Bar was simply omitted. The unfortunate irony: The old-guard aesthetics for which the Plaza was always known have recently come back into vogue, while the Ian Schragerish aesthetics of the hotel's new features now look passé. Mercifully, the new owners kept the murals and woodwork intact in the historical Oak Room and Oak Bar, but one senses that the ghosts of the hotel's history have fled to choicer climes.

"THE PLAYERS" Instead of "the cast." Casts are for broken legs.

PLUMED HELMETS An insidious approach to warfare: Your opponents will die of laughter.

POCKETBOOKS Today's women are being crippled by oversize shoulder bags and (so-called) handbags. Why is it that our grandmothers made out just fine with their neat little pocketbooks, and we have to lug our lives around with us everywhere? The hardware alone on our it-bags is heavy enough to cripple a bull. Also: Pocketbooks are good for whacking uppity suitors and would-be muggers.

POCKET WATCHES They used to be the most meaningful heirloom a father could pass on to his son, as you may remember from *Pulp Fiction*.

fig. 24: TIME ERASES ALL WOUNDS

POETRY   *You say it never went out of style,*
              I say that you're living in denial.

POISON-PENNED THEATER CRITICS Dorothy Parker is usually cited as the most delightfully vicious drama critic in modern history; as her biographer Marion Meade wrote, "Theatrical producers viewed her as a piranha and dreaded the sight of her tiptoeing down the aisles." Yet my favorite wicked critic is fictional: Waldo Lydecker (played by Clifton Webb) in the 1944 film *Laura*, in which he boasts: "I don't use a pen. I write with a goose quill dipped in venom."

POISON Poisoning a person is a much more elegant way to murder him than shoving him down the stairs or shooting him. There used to be a real art to poisoning; a veritable industry of blackhearted apothecaries and witch doctors languished when it went out of fashion.

I recently came across an exciting book in a vintage cookbook store called *Cooking to Kill: The Poison Cookbook*. The cover featured a spice cabinet with a jar of "arsenic" nestled in between the marjoram and rosemary jars; "cyanide" resided sweetly between the basil and thyme. "Anyone can kill vulgarly," declared the introduction. "But we should be above the brutal, the direct, the unappetizing approach. This little book will teach you to tickle the palates of your guests . . . [as they] take off for the Great Adventure with the taste of your superlative cooking still on their lips!"

I was dismayed to learn that the book was satirical, but it was inspiring all the same.

POLAROID CAMERAS A happy medium between the lush results of film and the instant gratification of digital cameras.

POLKA DOTS Old-fashioned but cheerful: good for a Monday-blues dress.

POPOVERS A light, hollow roll made from an egg batter and a divine alternative to biscuits or bread at dinner. The popover's name was derived from the way the batter swells or "pops" over the muffin tin's top while baking. The following recipe is from *Public School Domestic Science* (1898) by Mrs. J. Hoodless:

POPOVERS

2 cups flour	3 eggs
2 cups milk	½ teaspoon salt

Beat the eggs (without separating) until very light, then add the milk and salt; pour this mixture on the flour (slowly), beating all the while. Beat until smooth and light, about five minutes. Grease gem pans or small cups, and bake in a moderately hot oven about thirty-five minutes. They should increase to four times their original size.

PORCELAIN SKIN Don't fool yourself: Self-tanning creams turn you tiger orange, and tanning beds are UV-ray coffins. A hundred years ago, tanned skin was considered vulgar and peasantlike among fashionable women, who strived for pale complexions. Until the sun-kissed "California girl" aesthetic came into fashion in the midtwentieth century, women religiously shielded their skin from the sun with hats, parasols, scarves, and gloves.

This all sounds suspiciously enlightened, but at the turn of the last century, a few women also did horrific things to achieve and maintain an aristocratic, tomblike pallor: Creams containing arsenic and mercury were popular, even though they often poisoned the blood of their users. Two other appalling beauty routines: the fin de siècle use of atropine (now used as a wartime anti-nerve-gas agent) eye drops to keep irises "alluringly" dilated; and tooth blackening with lead (an aristocratic practice with pre-Meiji Japanese women; black smiles were considered more elegant than ivory-colored teeth).

Deadly fashion: never in style.

POSTCARDS An emblem of faraway adventure, along with memento stickers for your traveling trunk. Especially lovely and quite rare today: postcards with scalloped edges.

POSTURE Next time you walk past a manicure salon, peek in the window at the women getting their nails done. I'll bet you a million bucks that they're all sullenly slumped down in their chairs, as though they'd been shot.

POTBELLY STOVES They're so jolly; it's like having a fat little chef in the kitchen with you.

POT-AU-FEU "ROYAL"

This now-uncommon, classic recipe is hundreds of years old, but I first came across it—reinterpreted by chef Roger Vergé—in 1975, when I was working at the wonderful Le Moulin de Mougins restaurant. Pot-au-Feu "Royal" is a boiled meat extravaganza in four services. From one course to the next, the textures and flavors develop, progressing from a light, ethereal first course to a rich, complex, and hearty last bite. But every course is indulgent and worthy of celebration.

Here is my take on the classic:

1. A taste of game birds: partridge, pheasant, and quail in a wild mushroom consommé with whole poached foie gras, served with sourdough toast and shaved black truffle.

2. A taste of charcuterie *au chou:* ham hock, *cervelas* sausage with pistachio, pork belly, and pig cheeks, served in a light pork broth with cabbage, potato, and *mostarda di frutta.*

3. A taste of white meat: veal shank, veal tongue, calf's head, sweetbreads, and a poularde with zucchini, fennel, and butternut squash, finished with a cracked pepper, shallot, and *fines herbes* olive oil dressing.

4. A taste of dark meat: beef shank, whole marrow bone, short ribs, and a rare aiguillette of beef tenderloin, all with six root vegetables (carrot, celeriac, turnips, parsnips, rutabaga, and salsify) and spicy Dijon mustard.

—Daniel Boulud • **CHEF AND RESTAURATEUR**

POWDER PUFFS Big, luxurious, fluffy white or pink ones to dunk into tins of sweet-smelling talcum powder. The puff should sit like an exotic pet on your vanity table, waiting patiently in between uses.

POWDER ROOM And also the demure phrase "powdering my nose."

PRE-BRAZILIAN WAX AESTHETICS Brazilian waxes should have no part in a civilized culture. Historically speaking, men seemed to have found women just as sexy before this criminal beauty fad gurgled up out of some witch's cauldron.

PRESSED FLOWERS Take several of your favorite flowers and press them between two sheets of wax paper; when ironed, this turns into a sort of stained-glass memento. Pressed-flower diaries are a charming way to document a bucolic holiday.

PRINCESS PHONES

Every living room needs a Karl Springer telephone table perched next to a swanky sofa. Talking on a proper phone puts the glamour back into technology and somehow makes a house feel like a home. It's impossible to feel kittenish whilst yammering away on a cell phone.

—*Jonathan Adler* • INTERIOR DECORATOR

PRINTER'S DEVILS This job title sounds far more nefarious than it actually was: Printer's devils were apprentices at old-guard printing presses. I just love the idea of handing out a business card bearing the words "Printer's Devil."

SOME FAMOUS AMERICANS WHO WERE PRINTER'S DEVILS
IN THEIR EARLY YEARS OF EMPLOYMENT:

Benjamin Franklin

Warren Harding

Mark Twain

Walt Whitman

John Kellogg *(of breakfast cereal fame)*

PROFILE PORTRAITS I don't mean the social Web site variety; rather, I'm referring to the painted Medici-era variety that have totally fallen out of fashion today. Inspired by ancient coins and medallions, paintings of a sitter's profile were particularly popular in Italy between 1450 and 1500. Some people consider a profile portrait haughty and inaccessible, but an individual's profile is often his or her most distinguishing angle, and can therefore be very telling.

PROMENADES Promenading used to be a very important pastime, especially in Paris: The well born and well dressed would stroll on certain well-appointed promenades to see and be seen by other illustrious members of society; both ladies and gentlemen of means had special promenade wardrobes. A return of promenade culture in some form would be a most refreshing antidote to the car culture in which we currently live.

PROVERBS A distant cousin to the cliché—but in many instances, both clichés and old proverbs still ring true. For instance, who can argue against the wisdom of the following?

> *A chain is only as strong as its weakest link.*
> *A fool and his money are soon parted.*
> *Don't put all your eggs in one basket.*
> *Birds of a feather flock together.*
> *You can't get blood from a stone.*
> *You catch more flies with honey than with vinegar.*
> *Empty vessels make the most noise.*
> *Handsome is as handsome does.*
> *People who live in glass houses shouldn't throw stones.*
> *You can't make a silk purse from a sow's ear.*
> *He who pays the pipers chooses the tune.*

See also AESOP'S FABLES

"PUDGY PIE" Actually, this is just an endearing Depression-era name for what we call "paninis" today. A compressed toasted cheese sandwich, pudgy pies used to be made over an open fire in an iron that shaped the final result into a plump, round shape (hence the name "pudgy pie"). The irons were also called "hobo pie irons," since these delicacies could be easily made on the road over an improvised campfire.

PUNCH BOWLS Punch bowls are the Lolitas of serving ware: Filled with pink party punch, they look dainty and sweet and innocent but portend all sorts of naughty behavior. They used to be the heart and soul of the party; now hardly anyone has them in their cupboards anymore. Usually made from crystal or cut glass, they often came in sets that included ladles and matching punch cups that could hang from the bowl's edge on little removable hooks.

See also WHIRLIGIG PUNCH

QUALITY OVER QUANTITY Buy better, buy less: a notion that is mercifully staging a comeback at last. But we also remain in an epoch of fast fashion, fast food, and disposable technology—so temptations to digress from this wise mantra are everywhere.

QUILLS AND INK Sometimes not even a fountain pen will do the trick. Some of the most beautiful calligraphy comes from quills, and they are surprisingly easy to track down and use. Use them for wedding invitations, dinner menus, and love letters.

fig. 25: MIGHTIER THAN THE SWORD

QUIZZING GLASSES Also called *lorgnettes*, quizzing glasses were a small nineteenth-century cross between a spyglass and a magnifying glass. Their use? The close and unashamed scrutiny of one's rivals, comrades, and other creatures at the theater or while promenading. A newcomer would emerge at one of the opera hall entrances, and suddenly everyone would whip out his or her quizzing glass, which had been squirreled away in a hat or a feathered fan. They became so faddish that manufacturers of snuffboxes began to add small *lorgnette* compartments.

Take a quizzing glass to a local outdoor café early one Sunday morning and peer through it at any of your neighbors who might be doing a walk of shame; whip it out during a ladies luncheon and examine the Botox gone awry. The quizzing glass will make you very knowledgeable and *very* popular.

RABANNE, PACO (B. 1934) Whether you love or hate him, you can't deny that he was intensely creative in his heyday. Rabanne originally studied to become an architect but instead became the *enfant terrible* of the fashion world in the 1960s. Taking a cue from the contemporaneous Pop Art movement, he made wild dresses out of chain mail, aluminum panels, and plastic; in 1966 he showed a collection of "12 Experimental and Unwearable Dresses in Contemporary Materials." Anteceding today's concept of so-called disposable fashion by decades, he marketed paper dresses sold in envelopes. If you want to see some of his opinionated creations in person, go to the New York Vintage on Manhattan's 25th Street and ask to see the Rabannes in the "borrowing only" collection.

RADIO DRAMAS A picture may be worth a thousand words, but radio plays let the imagination run wild. For example, on October 30, 1938, millions of listeners heard radio news alerts of a violent Martian attack on Earth; many ran out of their homes screaming while others packed up their cars and fled. What they were *really* hearing: Orson Welles's radio adaptation of H. G. Wells's novel *The War of the Worlds*. The incident merited the *New York Times'* top headline the next day:

Radio Listeners in Panic, Taking War Drama as Fact

Many Flee Homes to Escape 'Gas Raid' From Mars–Phone Calls Swamp Police at Broadcast of Wells Fantasy

READING ALOUD Not just to children; my dad still used to read out loud from Sherlock Holmes after dinner when I visited home during my college years.

REAL SOCIALITES Socialites of yesteryear entertained and *exuded* exclusivity; many of today's so-called socialites attend nightly rounds of "parties" at stores celebrating dubious product launches. Oh, the *glamour.*

RECEIVING LINES A civilized wedding ritual: It ensures that you get at least *some* face time with each of your guests, who might feel neglected otherwise. President Theodore Roosevelt's New Year's Day receiving lines at the White House were particularly famous, most notably for the gusto of the receiver himself:

> He seizes on the fingers of every guest, and wrings them with surprising power. "It's a full and very firm grip," warns one newspaper, "that might bring a woman to her knees if she wore her rings on her right hand." . . . This lightning moment of contact is enough for him to transmit the full voltage of his charm.
>
> —Excerpt from *The Rise of Theodore Roosevelt* (1979) by Edmund Morris

RECIPES NAMED AFTER ROYALTY A few examples of old favorites:

CHERRIES JUBILEE

Made of flambéed cherries and liqueur and topped with vanilla ice cream, this dessert was created by Chef Auguste Escoffier to honor Queen Victoria's Diamond Jubilee in 1897.

STRAWBERRIES ROMANOV

There is more than one legend about this dessert's origin, although one popular theory states that this concoction of whipped cream and strawberries soaked in orange-flavored liqueur was made for Russian Czar Nicholas I by chef Antonin Carême (who also made soufflés flecked with real gold for the Rothschilds in Paris, and had the honor of baking Napoleon's wedding cake). Traditional versions of the dish call for a heavy cream topping that incorporates sour cream and vanilla.

TEXT CONTINUES NEXT PAGE ⟫→

OYSTERS ROCKEFELLER

Because America has had its royalty too, and still does. This very rich dish was created in 1899 at the famed New Orleans restaurant Antoine's for the equally rich John D. Rockefeller. Oysters on the half shell are topped with a special sauce and bread crumbs, and then baked in a pan filled with hot salt. Antoine's closely guards its recipe; the great-grandson of the dish's creator once cryptically wrote that "the sauce is basically a purée of a number of green vegetables other than spinach."

It is amusing to speculate about what the desserts of today's leaders could be called. Would we get, for example, "Bubba Cake" in honor of Bill Clinton, or "Arugula Obama" in honor of our forty-fourth president?

RED CABOOSES ON TRAINS Like an exclamation point at the end of a long, Jamesian sentence.

RED LIPSTICK There was a time when no woman would leave home without wearing it—just as men would not leave the house hatless. Several swipes of red lipstick bring instant glamour, instant presentation.

REPORTERS' NOTEBOOKS These slender, pocket-size, beige note-books with spiraled tops acquired the patina of heirlooms; these days, reporter's notes often go straight to Twitter and other such Web sites—as if notes count as vetted facts.

REVUES These nineteenth- and early-twentieth-century multi-act theater productions—featuring a mix of dancing, singing, and other performances—would be perfect for today's short attention spans.

RIDDLES For those of you who are weary of hosting family holiday gather-ings: Refuse to serve any food until your guests can solve a riddle of your choosing. It will be *automatically* suggested that someone else host the next Thanksgiving.

[PLATE 15]

fit for a king

THE RIVIERA Let's somehow magically bring back the unblemished, beautiful French Riviera described in Lost Generation literature and memoirs, as embodied by Villa America in the 1920s. Its owners, Sara and Gerald Murphy (two "moderately wealthy and irrepressibly sociable Jazz Age American expatriates," as the *New Yorker* once called them) bought this seaside chalet (which they called Villa America) in Cap d'Antibes in 1923—which was then still undiscovered and unblemished by keen *bon ton* resort-goers.

Villa America almost single-handedly changed that—and also popularized sunbathing and beach picnics, virtually unknown activities at the time. In the mornings, Gerald would go down to the beach and rake away the seaweed and do exercises with the three Murphy children. Life was simple and all about salt and sun and food. This summery Riviera wholesomeness attracted the attentions of the Murphys' most glamorous friends: Over the years, Villa America welcomed everyone "who counted in adventurous art and literature," according to the same *New Yorker* profile, including Picasso, photographer Man Ray, poet Archibald MacLeish, writer and critic Dorothy Parker, F. Scott and Zelda Fitzgerald, and Ernest Hemingway.

I guess there's a downside of showing too many famous people too good a time; soon, everyone else wants to join the party, and eventually you end up with the jammed-packed Riviera we have today.

ROCKING CHAIRS Especially on porches. Rocking chairs are the most soothing form of self-administered therapy ever.

fig. 26: BETTER THERAPY
THAN THE COUCH

ROLLER SKATES Those white ones with red laces and keys are devastatingly chic. In the late 1970s, I had some metal skates that you strapped to your shoes; they were throwbacks even then. I'm told that in the '50s, replacement skate keys cost 25¢ to replace; this was a lot of money then (five ice cream sundaes, in kid-world), so children made damn sure not to lose their keys.

ROLLTOP DESKS When closed, rolltop desks look like they're housing all sorts of secrets.

ROMAN AND GREEK GODS They were always up to something naughty.

ROOF GARDENS

From the 1880s to the 1920s, the skyline of midtown Manhattan was dotted with a series of amazing outdoor gathering places: landscaped roof gardens, ablaze with lights and open to the evening air, where New Yorkers and visitors strolled across lavishly landscaped terraces, through constructed fantasy environments (a European village, a Dutch farm), and into big, airy greenhouselike canopies, under whose lacy metal frameworks hundreds of customers could sit at a time. There were bars and seating areas, promenades from which guests could peer ten or twelve floors down to the bustling city below, outdoor band shells, and theaters where patrons could enjoy summertime musical shows and variety acts.

And, of course, open-air dance floors, where bands in white tie played the latest hits and couples spun around the floor with nothing but the stars above and the muted sounds of the city below. It was the perfect warm-weather entertainment in the era before air-conditioning, when evening breezes made the high roofs of the city the coolest place in town. But it was also the most magical and urbane public environment imaginable—glittering, magical realms, poised a hundred feet or more above the sidewalk, filled with the lilt of a foxtrot, the laughter of the crowd, the clink of champagne flutes under the moonlight.

— *James Sanders* • ARCHITECT, AUTHOR OF *CELLULOID SKYLINE: NEW YORK AND THE MOVIES*

ROPE-PULLED DOORBELLS Announce your arrival with majesty.

ROSIE THE RIVETER During World War II, "Rosie the Riveter" was one of the best-known symbols of the U.S. government's propaganda campaign encouraging women to join the war effort. Widespread male enlistment left a huge dearth of manpower in essential industries such as airplane and munitions production, and—thanks to Rosie's ubiquitous image—nearly 3 million women came to work in defense plants.

Rosie appeared in a variety of guises, depending on who was drawing her; one of the more famous images portrays her flexing one of her biceps, her neat up-do wrapped in a polka-dotted handkerchief; at the bottom of the poster appears the phrase "We Can Do It!" An interpretation by famed American artist Norman Rockwell shows a brawny, overall-clad Rosie seated with a piece of machinery in her lap, calmly eating a sandwich with her feet planted firmly on Hitler's manifesto *Mein Kampf*; a huge American flag flutters in the background.

While we may not have specific need of munitions-factory Rosies right now, her gritty message—roll up your sleeves and get to work, without whining or primness—will always be valuable during times of duress.

ROTARY-DIAL TELEPHONES They make it harder to drunk-dial an old flame (or would-be new flame) in the middle of the night.

ROUGE The word just sounds so wonderfully tawdry, as opposed to "blush," which sounds so virginal. A "broad" would wear rouge.

RUBBER-BAND BALLS A good, grandmotherly way to store rubber bands, to keep them from forming a tangled snake pit in your junk drawer. Also a delightful toy for kids, because it bounces in odd directions. Start with a golf ball or Ping-Pong ball, and just keep winding rubber bands around it until it's big and fat.

RUSSELL, ROSALIND (1907–1976) Perhaps best known as Hollywood's rendition of literary character Auntie Mame, but a thousand times more sublime as wisecracking ace reporter Hildy Johnson in *His Girl Friday*. That movie should be mandatory viewing material for every young girl and *all* aspiring journalists.

RUSSIAN ICONS These evocative depictions of Russian saints and religious figures were often painted on wood, with ornate panels of gold or silver sometimes layered on top. I've always liked the idea of vaguely haunted or mystical paintings: I was told once in a museum that if you stare at one long enough, a Russian icon will "draw you in" or hypnotize you.

Many icons are likely more haunted by strange turns in history than by traditional spirits: in the 1920s and '30s, the Soviet government raised funds for their treasury by selling off many of these priceless works to Western tourists.

SACK SUITS They've become synonymous with legendary actor Cary Grant—who wore loose suits as elegantly as Fred Astaire wore his tails. In the 1930s especially, sacks suits became a symbol of the casual sportiness for which America has always been known. Today our eyes are trained to favor a more fitted silhouette; yet a beautifully tailored sack suit can denote a certain breeziness that a tighter suit cannot.

SADDLE SHOES Worn by women, they carry a hint of childlike innocence, a whiff of sporty masculinity, and practicality combined with devil-may-care insouciance. It's no wonder, then, that Old Hollywood stars like Marlene Dietrich—who projected an image combining virgin, whore, Victor, and Victoria all at once—made sure that they were photographed wearing them.

SAFARI HATS Sometimes called "sun helmets," safari hats manage to look silly and romantic at the same time. Have a look at that wonderful, famous photograph of Teddy Roosevelt depicted on his famous jaunt down a treacherous, unmapped, rapids-choked tributary of the Amazon River wearing a mosquito-net-swathed sun helmet and fringed hand gauntlets as he wrote his nightly *Scribner's* articles. Under assault from local natives, piranhas, and all sorts of unspeakable insects, he appears as serene as a Buddha under the brim of that hat.

SAILOR PANTS High-waisted, wide-legged white ones with a double row of navy or red buttons up the stomach. Very 1940s, very jaunty, and very flattering.

SALONS Forums for the exchange of ideas. Or a place to pick a few up if you are in short supply.

SALOONS Sometimes you just *need* to see a good bar fight.

THE ORIGINAL SALTAIR Built in 1893 and billed as "the Coney Island of the West," this magnificent Moorish palace of a resort appeared to be a mirage on the glistening edge of the Great Salt Lake in Utah. Onion domes topped various colonnaded towers; palms filled the main courtyard. When its patrons weren't bobbing like corks in the lake's ultra-salty waters, they could be found dining in one of the picnic pavilions or dancing on what was advertised as the world's largest dance floor. Saltair burned down at the peak of its popularity in 1925; subsequent resorts built on the spot have succumbed to fire and floods as well.

SASHES Belts are everywhere again, but one rarely sees sashes anymore. One benefit that you get with a sash but not a belt: At any moment, you can whip off a jersey sash and wind it into a turban.

SATIN CHAISE LOUNGES Very Old Hollywood. Especially lovely and decadent in the bathroom; best enjoyed while lounged upon while donning a marabou-fringed chiffon robe.

SATIN EVENING SLIPPERS Each pair exudes the promise of a night of dancing, and the most exquisite hangover the next morning.

SATIN PAJAMAS They became a badge of the newly liberated woman in the first half of the twentieth century, along with other innocuous-by-today's-standards objects like bicycles. Pajamas had been strictly menswear; yet in the 1920s, white satin or silk separates became all the rage for stylish urban women. The sensuous garments (often referred to as "lounging pajamas") carried with them the delicious taboo of appropriating an item from the masculine sphere for female use.

A set of such pajamas were—and remain—*far* sexier than the cheap lace dental-floss teddies that one finds at Victoria's Secret these days.

"SCANTIES" Particularly apt today, since "scanties" (i.e., underpants) are so scant among example-setting young starlets.

SCARVES IN DRESSING ROOMS Elegant retailers used to have a silk scarf hanging in each dressing room; you'd put it over your head as you tried on clothing, to protect your hair and makeup and keep your lipstick from soiling the clothes.

SCAT SINGING It can be as electrifying as the most dramatic operatic solo.

SCENTED INK It makes letter writing even more personalized, as a perfumed extension of yourself.

SCHIAPARELLI, ELSA (1890–1973) This lavishly creative designer—known as "Schiap" to her friends—was once as revered and famous as Coco Chanel, who referred to her rival as "that Italian artist who makes clothes."

Schiaparelli was closely associated with the Dada and Surrealist movements, collaborating on pieces and collections with artists Salvador Dalí, Jean Cocteau, and Alberto Giacometti; her most famous creation was arguably the Lobster Dress, a simple white silk evening gown with a big, fat, insouciant lobster painted by Dali onto the skirt. It was worn by several of the era's most fashionable women; Wallis Simpson donned it in a series of now-iconic photographs taken by Cecil Beaton just before her controversial marriage to Edward VIII. Always irreverent about fashion, Schiaparelli also created a hat shaped like a woman's high-heeled shoe, with the heel pointing straight up into the air and the toe tilted over the wearer's forehead. It too was touted by some of the world's most formidable clotheshorses.

I love Schiaparelli for many reasons, but above all because one day she just decided to become a designer; with no formal training, she simply drew up innovative clothing sketches and had local tailors create them. Among her offerings: sweaters with x-ray-style rib cages printed over the wearer's actual ribs—a shockingly insouciant design at the time, but department store buyers loved them, and so did their customers.

I love the message behind Schiaparelli's rise, comparable to the way Athena sprang from Zeus's skull, fully grown and shimmering in battle armor: Visualize what you want to be, and *become* it.

See also SURREALISM

SCHRAFFT'S Once ubiquitous in the Northeast, Schrafft's was an empire of soda-fountain restaurants and a pop-culture household name. Andy Warhol did a TV spot for it: "The chocolate sundae," proclaimed the credit line rolling diagonally across the screen, "was photographed for Schrafft's by Andy Warhol." The chain got a mention in *Auntie Mame*; W. H. Auden wrote a poem called "In Schrafft's" that was later set to music by the composer Richard Wilson. In the 1961 film *Breakfast at Tiffany's*, Audrey Hepburn is eating a pastry from a Schrafft's restaurant bag; in homage, Paramount released an Audrey Hepburn *Breakfast at Tiffany's* doll that included a Schrafft's bakery bag and coffee cup among its accessories.

While there were once reportedly dozens of Schrafft's locations around New York City, all evidence of this once-iconic chain appears to have been effaced from the cityscape.

SCHUMANN, CLARA (1819–1896) A brilliant pianist and composer, German-born Clara Schumann was celebrated during the nineteenth century as an astonishing prodigy; at eighteen, the Austrian emperor named her "Royal and Imperial Chamber Virtuosa," an unprecedented accolade for someone of her age and gender (her nickname at court: "Wundermädchen," or "Wonder girl"). Not surprisingly, Schumann also became a muse to other virtuosos—namely her husband, composer Robert Schumann, and later, composer Johannes Brahms. Yet today her work (and memory) has been largely occluded by her husband's—making Clara something of a "Shakespeare's sister," as Virginia Woolf envisioned this fictional "sister" to be: a woman of enormous talent who is prevented from achieving greatness by societal conventions and domestic responsibilities.

SEALING WAX A dramatic way to end the writing of a letter: You get to light a stick of wax aflame, let big blood-red drops spatter the back of the envelope, and finish with a mighty *thump* of the stamp onto the wax.

SECRET WATCHES A wonderful Victorian contribution to female adornment: a bracelet with a watch face hidden in its facade, usually behind some sort of tiny, secret hinged door. This is a particularly favorite item of mine: I personally have always disliked wearing watches; it makes one look so dreadfully efficient.

"SEEDY" Meaning disreputable, run-down, or degraded: usually used in conjunction with the word "hotel."

SELF-ADMINISTERED MANICURES Getting salon manicures used to be considered a splurge for special occasions; these days, many women get "manis" as often as once a week. All of that cuticle snipping often makes your fingers look worse, and many of the quickie salons polluting every city corner are grossly unhygienic, passing warts, infections, and all sorts of unspeakable afflictions onto their patrons.

Manicures became big business with the twentieth-century rise of the cosmetics industry and used to be a sign of social standing, indicating that the owner of those highly polished talons had plenty of leisure time and was exempt from housework and other manual labors. In the 1920s and '30s, ladies often left the moons and the tips of their nails unlacquered, until cosmetics titan Helena Rubinstein reportedly instructed women to paint the whole nail and ushered in a new aesthetic that remains popular to this day.

Here are some instructions on how to reproduce an at-home 1930s "vintage" manicure, excerpted from an old magazine editorial:

> File nails into an almond, oval, or long-tapered shape. Soak fingers in water, push back cuticles, and massage in cuticle oil. Remove excess oil with varnish remover. Paint on one coat of hardener. Once dry, add French strips to the moons and tips of nails. Paint two coats of your chosen color and add a final coat of hardener for longevity. Dry completely and remove the strips.

And lo! You shall have hands that rival Rita Hayworth's.

OLD-FASHIONED SELTZER BOTTLES They looked beautiful on bars and café tables, and made such a festive *hiss* as you squirted the seltzer into your highball glass.

"SEM" (1863–1934) George Goursat—whose work appeared under the pseudonym "Sem"—was a devilish Belle Epoque caricaturist who stylishly skewered members of France's political elite and fashionable society. Coco Chanel once contended that Picasso's caricatures (his best works, in her opinion) were copied from Sem. Yet like so many members of the decadent *fin de siècle* art scene, Goursat left the party behind once World War I began to ravage the continent; he swapped out Maxim's for the front line, on which he reported as a war correspondent.

There is a wonderful gallery of Sem's naughty caricatures at Doubles, a private club in Manhattan's Sherry Netherland hotel. Look for a "secret" door in the hotel's lobby and quietly slip through: On the other side, you'll find a long stairway leading to the underground club, its walls lined with wonderful Goursat portraits of people who lived and mattered long ago.

SEPARATE OVENS Many kitchens used to feature two separate ovens, one on top of the other, so you could bake two different things at different temperatures at the same time. It's curious that this intensely practical convenience is no longer common.

SEPIA-TONED PHOTOGRAPHS They can infuse even the most insignificant of events—and the events' participants—with retrospective poignancy and a look of historical significance.

SERENADES Even if you can't sing to save your life: It's the thought that counts.

fig. 27: PITCH PERFECT

SERVICE Today the idea that "the customer is always right" appears to be as dead as the person often credited with coining the phrase: department store founder Harry Gordon Selfridge Sr. (1858–1947). Surliness is the new "service with a smile."

SHAVING KITS FOR MEN With horsehair whisks and brushes, and wood- or silver-handled razors that are passed down through generations.

fig. 28: LATHER UP

SHERBET In recent years, sherbet has been supplanted by its hoity-toity cousin, sorbet. The difference: sorbet is basically fruit juice and shaved ice, while sherbet contains milk and has a texture that evokes ice cream and cotton candy.

SHERRY There is nothing more charming than tiny sherry glasses. I'm partial to cutlery and tableware of unlikely proportions.

SHOO-FLY PIE This pie falls into the "fun to say to the waitress" category; it was created by early settlers of Pennsylvania Dutch country, who often had to rely on stashes of long-lasting nonperishable staples, including flour, brown sugar, molasses, lard, salt, and spices. This list just happens to comprise the main ingredients of shoo-fly pie, a make-do concoction made by resourceful settler women. Here's a delightful recipe from Maple Springs Farm (www.maplespringsfarm.com), nestled in the dairy country of north-central Pennsylvania:

SHOO-FLY PIE

1 cup flour
¾ cup brown sugar
1 heaping tablespoon Crisco
1 cup King Syrup
1 teaspoon baking soda

¾ cup boiling water
1 beaten egg
One 10-inch uncooked
pie shell

Preheat oven to 375. Mix flour, brown sugar, and shortening into crumbs. Split the crumb mixture in half. Set one half aside for crumbs.

SILK STOCKINGS With seams up the backs: sheer luxury—literally. Silk stockings used to be given as mistress gifts, along with chocolates and roses and that sort of thing.

SILVER DOLLARS You're less likely to trade precious dollars for an unneeded Starbucks latte if they're made out of silver.

SILVER PALATE A line of cookbooks popular in the 1980s; the old girls who wrote them were likely to cut a stick of butter into a *salad*, but that was always the beauty of the enterprise. Pick up an old copy of *The Silver Palate Good Times Cookbook*, buy a vat of heavy cream, and make the chicken breasts in champagne sauce, the golden caviar soufflé, or the smoked salmon and cream cheese soup.

SILVER STREAMERS AT NEW YEAR'S EVE The sort that come in coils; you hold one end and throw the rest into the air, releasing the most pleasing stream of gleaming silver. The sight of a room absolutely strewn with shimmering silver is a lovely way to behold the New Year.

Pour the King Syrup in the other half of the crumb mixture. Mix the baking soda in the boiling water. When this fizzes, pour on top of the King Syrup/crumb mixture. If the soda water doesn't fizz, you didn't get your water hot enough or your baking soda is bad. Dump out water and try again. Pie won't rise if it doesn't fizz. Add 1 beaten egg. Mix with fork.

Pour in unbaked pie shell. If you don't want to make your own shell, just use one of those fold-out Pillsbury ones. Top with crumbs. Bake in preheated oven. Bake 10 minutes. Don't open the door, turn oven down to 350. Bake an additional 30–40 minutes.

. . . .

ANOTHER VITAL BUT UNMENTIONED INGREDIENT:
BUZZING FLIES TO SHOO AWAY.

SILVER TEA SETS Their fineness will raise the tone—and caliber—of gossip that takes place during teatime.

SILVER TOAST STANDS Breakfast is often treated as the poor relation of meals, when it should arguably be the most elegant meal of the day, since it sets the tone for the hours ahead. Pour orange juice from a glass or crystal pitcher; serve toast in a old-fashioned silver toast stand.

SIMPLE WEDDING RINGS Today's ring fingers are laden with hardware: A typical arrangement includes a chunky engagement ring with the diamond hovering practically an *inch* above one's finger, a matching gem-encrusted wedding band, topped off with "anniversary" or "celebration" bands stacked on at every opportunity. These dubious gewgaws are less a symbol of affection or status than a badge of your susceptibility to Tiffany & Co.'s marketing machine. Understatement is sometimes the biggest statement of all.

SKATING PARTIES These once-popular diversions were often followed by a post–skating party supper; here is a sample menu from the 1966 edition of *The New York Times Menu Cook Book*:

A Supper After a Skating Party

Hot Buttered Rum

Old-Fashioned Vegetable Soup

Crusty French Bread

Mixed Green Salad

Cranberry Cheese Cupcakes

"SLATTERN" I adore words that sound like what they mean, like "zing" and so on. "Slattern" most certainly falls into that category.

slat•tern \'slad-ərn\ *n* **1** : a slovenly, untidy woman or girl **2** : a slut; harlot

"Harlot" is quite wonderful too; it sounds so dismissive and indignant. As in, "Oh, don't pay a *scrap* of attention to that harlot."

SLEEPER BERTHS ON AIRPLANES Despite their expense, today's first-class compartments strongly resemble dingy office cubicles; one needs a proper little room with a bed and a wall of curtains, where you can cold-cream your face and slap a couple of cucumber slices on your eyelids.

"SLIMMING REGIME" It's curious how words related to the torture of weight loss always have such dire undertones: *die*-t, reducing regimen, slimming *regime*. One might as well call it as it is.

SMELLING SALTS An antebellum alternative to Red Bull.

SMITH, BESSIE (EARLY 1890S–1937) Billie Holiday seems to be enjoying quite a renaissance, but you don't often hear Bessie—the gravel-voiced, cantankerous, oversexed "Empress of the Blues"—on café playlists and such.

Born in Chattanooga to a part-time Baptist preacher father, Smith was orphaned at a young age. She began singing on the streets for money, eventually becoming a vaudeville sensation and then recording more than 160 tracks with Columbia. When Smith died in a car accident en route to a club date, seven thousand people swarmed her coffin at the funeral. Yet her grave remained unmarked until 1970, when a tombstone was finally purchased by her former housekeeper, Juanita Green, and singer Janis Joplin, who once reportedly said that Bessie's singing "showed me the air and taught me how to fill it."

TEXT CONTINUES NEXT PAGE ⟫→

One of my favorite, hilariously dirty, Bessie Smith songs is "Empty Bed Blues," which extols the amorous talents of her latest lover:

> *He's a deep sea diver with a stroke that can't go wrong*
> *He can stay at the bottom and his wind holds out so long*

... and "Need a Little Sugar in My Bowl," whose lyrics are a little too naughty to print here. All of her songs are best listened to on record players, with the accompanying crackles and pops.

See also LIMERICKS

SMOKE-FILLED JAZZ CLUBS AND PARISIAN CAFÉS
In such places, atmosphere is everything. Even if you hate the smell of cigarette smoke, you can't deny that it lends authenticity to the experience.

SNUFFBOXES Contemporary men have so few adornments. Snuffboxes used to be stylish, must-have gentleman's accessories; one prominent nineteenth-century English dandy, Viscount Petersham, had a different ornate snuffbox for each day of the year. Now they're just another outmoded object.

Snuff boxes usually fit in the palm of one's hand and carried powdered inhaling tobacco. They could be deeply elaborate in their designs, including one popular, charming model topped with a bird that rotated in a circle on the top of the box, sang, and flapped its metallic wings.

SONGBIRD PIES In which the songbirds fly out when the crust is cut: a highly unexpected way to honor a birthday; a whimsical alternative to a girl jumping out of a cake.

SOUVENIR CAMERA VIEWFINDERS The sort with rotating celluloid pictures of the world's great landmarks, such as the Leaning Tower of Pisa, the Sphinx, Niagara Falls, Big Ben, and so on. Kaleidoscopes held a similar hours-of-peering fascination.

SPATS For some reason, cartoon gangsters and villains are often drawn wearing them. The heighth of fashion for men throughout the 1920s, these jaunty little white shoe coverings usually have a neat little row of tiny black buttons running up the inseam. They would look very smart covering the tops of today's women's lace-up heeled booties or patent stilettos.

SPEAKEASIES Real ones—as opposed to the trendy faux speakeasies that have cropped up in New York City recently. Real speakeasies, or "speaks," were often dumps. In her memoir, Diana Vreeland describes evenings at the Abbaye, a "bottle club" frequented by both New York City's bon ton and gangsters alike. You'd arrive at an unmarked door, where an eye glaring through a peephole would greet you; once admitted, you'd descend a long flight of stairs into a cavernous little room where your liquor was served to you in bouillon cups.

"Bouillon, bouillon, bouillon—there was no *end* to the bouillon," Vreeland recalls.

If the lights went on and off three times, you gulped your "bouillon" down and hid your flask; the cops had arrived. Vreeland describes one night when there was a gangland shooting outside the Abbaye's door; pools of blood stained the ladies' satin dancing slippers red as they fled.

A wonderful surviving speakeasy: the '21' Club in New York City. When you're next there for a luncheon, ask the *maître d'* to tour the cellar, where the club's alcohol was stashed during Prohibition. Perhaps the most elaborately disguised vault in New York City, the entrance to the cellar was (and remains) practically invisible; the perfectly camouflaged 5,000-pound door appears to be part of a brick wall; in the 1920s, a shelved wall filled with canned goods stood in front, with several smoked hams dangling in front of *that*. The key to the door: a meat skewer, inserted into a tiny, innocuous-looking hole in the cement wall/door. Once heaved open, the door revealed two thousand cases of wine.

"SPECTACLES" The word "glasses" has very nerdy overtones:

> *Men seldom make passes*
> *At girls who wear glasses.*
> —Dorothy Parker

Yet the word "spectacles" sounds sweet and charming.

SPURS I hate it when people walk too closely behind me on the sidewalk. A good old-fashioned pair of cowboy spurs would likely solve that problem.

STANDING SHAVING MIRRORS A pre-plumbing bathroom accessory: These free-standing mirrors often had bowls for water and hooks for shaving whisks attached to their stands. Today they would make good on-the-go makeup stands for women as well.

STAR-GAZEY PIE Usually people aren't in a hurry to resurrect recipes from Old England, which was as notorious for its lumpy, starchy food as it was for its unfortunate dentistry. However, the whimsically named "star-gazey pie" is an amusing pleasure: Not for the faint of heart, star-gazey is a *very* old-fashioned Cornish fish pie in which fish heads jut through the piecrust, looking upward as though "star gazing." I don't know why I love the idea of this pie so much; in a children's book, the fish would have started talking or granting wishes.

If you're too squeamish to use fish heads, try having lobster heads poke through the crust of a lobster pot pie; that would be a nice Surrealist homage.

STEAMER TRUNKS Less practical now that there are such stingy luggage-weight restrictions on airplanes, but delightful regardless. The most beautiful sort are the vintage Louis Vuitton and Goyard ones. The second-nicest variety are the new Louis Vuitton and Goyard ones. When not in use, they make beautiful bedroom furniture when opened and standing on their sides. The old ones had little shelves and drawers, which look wonderful with strands of pearls and lace lingerie trailing out of them.

fig. 29: ALWAYS TIP YOUR PORTER HANDSOMELY

STEGOSAURUS These dinosaurs had such bold fashion sense with all of those beautiful, fierce plates.

See also RABANNE, PACO

"STINKO" As in, drunk as a skunk. An equally fun synonym: "blotto."

STRIPED BEACH AND POOL CABANAS Like little temples honoring the French Riviera and the Lido di Venezia in the 1920s.

May God strike down the linoleum-sided pool shed and other equally offensive poolside outbuildings.

THE STOCKS For egregious fashion offenders and overly loud cell-phone talkers.

THE STORK CLUB Influential gossip columnist Walter Winchell once called the Stork Club "the New Yorkiest spot in New York." Founded as a speakeasy in the 1920s, the Stork became the first and last word in the realm of elite supper-clubbing; *everyone* went there: Jack and Jackie, Marilyn and Joe, the Duke and Duchess (of Windsor, of course), Hemingway, Hitchcock, and Hoover. Despite all of this high-octane star power, my favorite thing about the Stork was that each little table sported a discreet back telephone, on which you could dial the other tables: *That* is a charming feature that we *need* to bring back.

Alas, this bastion of mirrored, velveted, crudité-d glamour closed in 1965— and today's urban populations have been left largely supper clubless.

STORYVILLE This infamous New Orleans red-light district invented new forms of decadence from around 1860 until 1917, when the federal government shut it down (over vigorous protest from the city government, according to one source). Considered by many to be the cradle of jazz (or at the very least, one of its most important incubators), most of Storyville's historic architecture—from its Victorian mansions to its tawdry shanties— was razed in the 1930s to make way for a public housing project.

[PLATE 16]

statement accessories

SUBVERSIVE PAMPHLETS Printed up in bright colors so no one missed them scattered about the streets and subways. They would make an excellent alternative to a boring old blog; it's easier than getting agented and cheaper than self-publishing a book.

SUGAR Like bread and butter: on Americans' blacklist. It's likely better to sweeten your tea with real sugar than metallic-tasting artificial sweetener; God only knows what that stuff will do to us in the long run.

SUITCASE RECORD PLAYERS They say all you need to travel is your credit card and your passport; I'd argue that the suitcase record player is the third must-take-along item. An adored friend of mine brings one with him practically everywhere—even on one trip to a secluded beach in Oman, where he could be spotted tenderly wiping sand from Fred Astaire records at sunrise.

SUITS OF ARMOR Good for covering up "fat" days, as long as you can squeeze yourself in to begin with.

SUNDAY "BEST" I like the idea of designating one day a week on which to dress up, even if you're the least religious person on the planet; it counter-balances the inanity of Casual Fridays.

SUPERSTITIONS We're so terribly rational and sensible these days. Black cats no longer produce the fear of God in us; we march right under ladders and don't even *notice* when the 13th falls on a Friday. Let's face it: Life is more fun with superstitions, even if they do turn everyday objects into emblems of terror. Don't forget that there's an upside to superstition as well: Heads-up pennies are still lucky, and finding a four-leaf clover will still make you rich.

SURREALISM My favorite Surrealist work was a Christmas gift from artist Salvador Dalí to comedian and harpist Arthur "Harpo" Marx: a harp with barbed-wire strings.

SUSPENDERS Rather adorable in red and when worn with Converse sneakers.

"SWASHBUCKLER" This archaic word means "a swaggering bully or ruffian." You're not supposed to like bullies or ruffians, but something about the word "swashbuckler" makes you want to invite one to a party.

"SWELL" This word is especially good in sarcastic use. "The toilet over-flowed? Oh, that's just *swell*."

SYLLABUB This largely forgotten English dessert seems like the ultimate comfort food: rich milk or cream whipped with sugar and lightly curdled with wine (for that extra-lulling effect).

There are many colorful vintage versions of this recipe. A household affairs author named Mrs. George W. M. Reynolds seemed determined to intoxicate all of London with a single cup of her boozy syllabub; her recipe in *The Household Book of Practical Receipts, in the Arts, Manufactures, and Trades, Including Medicine, Pharmacy, and Domestic Economy* (1871) instructs readers to mix together a pound of powdered sugar, the juice of four lemons, a quart of port, a quart of sherry, and one pint of brandy in a large bowl, and then "place the bowl under the cow, and milk it full." A "little rich cream" dollop went on top of the confection, as if to seal in the bacchanal of spirits.

Later versions had the consistency of whipped cream and were served in chilled parfait glasses, adorned with sprigs of mint and a dash of nutmeg. Lemon syllabub was particularly popular; it made a lovely spring or sum-mertime treat.

SYMBOLIC JEWELRY

While openly declaring your love can be sweet, symbolizing it can be so much more clever. The Victorian penchant for symbolism was wonderfully represented in their jewelry, and the subtle meanings hidden in pins, rings, and brooches must surely be brought back into our design vernacular. Set side by side, gemstones were used to spell out specific words; here are my favorite examples:

"DEAREST" Coded out using a Diamond, Emerald, Amethyst, Ruby, Emerald, Sapphire, and Topaz, set in that order.

"REGARDS" Ruby, Emerald, Garnet, Amethyst, Ruby, Diamond, and Sapphire.

Coiled serpents symbolized eternity and commitment; pearls stood for tears; floral motifs carried a deep range of meanings. A ring decorated with iris imagery, for instance, cryptically denoted "I have a message for you." The recipient would have to look inside the band for another hidden meaning. A primrose blossom meant "I can't live without you." The Victorians truly expressed the poignancy of love with a few simple blooms.

—*Lisa Salzer* • DESIGNER, LULU FROST JEWELRY

T with U

TABLE MANNERS In today's society, it's practically acceptable to let food fall out of your mouth onto the plate. The old song was right: "The fundamental things apply, as time goes by": mouth closed when chewing; elbows off the table and tucked in at your sides; napkin in your lap, folded in half; wait for the hostess to start eating before you tuck in. I highly recommend gifting *Tiffany's Table Manners for Teenagers* to egregious table-manners offenders of any age.

TABLEAUX VIVANTS Meaning "living pictures" in French, *tableaux vivants* featured costumed actors arranged as the subjects of a famous painting. In the nineteenth century, such highly stylized spectacles often provided the entertainment at society balls; sometimes several of the honored guests themselves comprised the tableaux.

Edith Wharton describes one such party in her novel *The House of Mirth*: A socially ambitious society doyenne prevails upon "a dozen fashionable women to exhibit themselves in a series of pictures" at the fête. The first tableau—which portrayed a "group of nymphs dancing across flower-strewn sward in the rhythmic postures of Botticelli's *Spring*"—stunned the attending crème de la crème of New York society. But the most mesmerizing tableau of all was created by the novel's tragic heroine, Lily Bart, whose pose as Sir Joshua Reynolds' painting *Mrs. Lloyd* drew gasps from the guests: "It was as though she had stepped, not out of, but into, Reynolds' canvas, banishing the phantom of his dead beauty by the beams of her living grace."

TABOR, ELIZABETH "BABY DOE" (1854–1935) The legendary young second bride of Colorado's "Silver King" Horace Tabor, beautiful Elizabeth "Baby Doe" rose to national infamy amid the most lavish of circumstances, and in time became one of the country's most astonishing riches-to-rags stories, now largely forgotten. The Tabors' 1883 wedding was attended by President Chester Arthur; Baby Doe's gown cost a reported $7,500, and her groom gifted her a $75,000 necklace that included the enormous "Isabella" diamond (which was allegedly sold by Spain's Queen Isabella to fund the Columbus expedition to the New World).

Denver society deemed the new bride a gold digger and snubbed the couple, but they lived a resplendent, extravagant lifestyle regardless. National fashion magazines and gossip columns followed Baby Doe's every move; her babies bore diamond-encrusted diaper pins. That is, until the 1893 silver crash devastated Tabor's fortune. Once one of America's great industrial barons, Horace was reduced to hauling slag from mines at $2.75 a day. He died in 1899, leaving his widow penniless. Baby Doe lived out her life in poverty, shivering in a shack next to her husband's repossessed "Matchless Mine," now water-filled; she froze to death there in 1935.

TAILORING In previous eras, buying new clothing meant fittings—*many* fittings. Diana Vreeland used to get three for her *nightgowns*. The process could be grueling—but the results were usually worth the hassle. If you look at 1940s and '50s clothing advertisements, everything was about *lines*, *silhouette*, and *tailoring*—and these components should still reign supreme.

Few Americans today realize how great an asset a tailor can be when it comes to perfecting their mass-produced wardrobes. A coat or suit or dress bought from Banana Republic or H&M can be vastly improved when adjusted to your measurements, or individualized with a few clever flourishes. When money is tight, your tailor is your new best friend. If you can't stand the sight of your tired old clothes but can't afford new ones, give your wardrobe a makeover. A tired pair of pinstriped slacks becomes a daring pair of shorts, to be worn over tights. An old fur jacket becomes a tunic, which looks great with a thick belt and leggings, and so on.

TEXT CONTINUES NEXT PAGE ⟫→

In eras past, ladies were advised to have a basic, versatile bespoke wardrobe custom made for them in the best fabrics they could afford; must-have pieces included:

- ••• A perfectly fitted black dress
- ••• A black or gray pencil skirt
- ••• A black or gray jacket that matches both the dress and skirt
- ••• A pair of flattering black trousers

The idea of custom-made clothing may sound indulgent, but the old girls were on to something: Investing in quality and versatility is always more cost-effective in the long run. As they knew, the fittings process forces you to evaluate what cuts and styles work best for you, and afterward you'll be less likely to make trend-driven impulse purchases. A gifted tailor will also flatter your physical assets and help mask your flaws; mass-market apparel isn't always so gracious.

Gentlemen: Menswear experts say that most of you are wearing your suits two sizes too big. That's like adding an extra thirty pounds to your frame without the fun of eating the food to gain it.

THE "TAKE ONE THING OFF" RULE There *can* be too much of a good thing, especially when it comes to accessories. Interior decorator and social powerhouse Elsie de Wolfe always used to make herself take one item off before she left the house: a bracelet, a necklace, whatever; it could have been a headband with a huge tulle bow in her case. This sage practice remains a good rule of thumb today; unless, of course, you are only wearing one thing to begin with.

TALCUM POWDER Formerly a central part of a lady's *toilette*; still very lovely on summer nights, after a bath, under a white linen nightgown, or sprinkled on white bed sheets.

TANGEE LIPSTICK This 1940s mainstay must-have lipstick is orange in the tube, goes on clear, and then "changes to complement your skin tone." A Web site that still sells Tangee features some heartwarming customer testimonials from women who wore the lipstick during the 1940s and '50s, and are just rediscovering it now:

> "When I was growing up my mother always wore Tangee lipstick, and many times when she applied it I would be standing near her. I am now sixty-seven years old and my mother has been gone for fifteen years. When I opened the tube of Tangee . . . the smell of it brought my mother's presence back to me. It was like she was standing right next to me. Thank you for this wonderful long-lost product, plus for bringing my mother back to me, if only for a second when I open the tube of Tangee."
>
> **—Ester, PALMYRA, VIRGINIA**

> "My first recollection of Tangee lipstick was at my great aunt's house in Greenville, South Carolina, in the late 1940s. They were two old maid sisters in their late 70s who lived together, and I loved to watch them curl their hair, which was very long, by putting a curling iron in the chimney of a kerosene lamp to heat it up. When they had their hair all fixed and were dressed up, they put on their Tangee lipstick and Tangee rouge and were ready to receive visitors out on the front porch on Sunday afternoons."
>
> **—Anne, HUNTSVILLE, ALABAMA**

TAP DANCING It's about as dated as dated can be, but tap dancing is still pretty astounding to behold when done by the old masters. Fred Astaire's soft shoe in *Top Hat* is one of the cinema's tenderest romantic gestures: In one scene, Ginger Rogers slumbers in a satin-filled hotel room directly below Astaire's; his energetic tap dancing jolts her awake. After being confronted by the great golden-haired beauty, Astaire spills sand from a (clean) ashtray onto the floor to soften the sound of his thundering taps; his subsequent dance is like a sweet, humorous lullaby.

TEA ROOMS They were like verbal tennis courts for gossipy women: You went to tea rooms to perfect your backhanded compliment.

TEA TIME

> "There are few hours in life more agreeable than the hour dedicated to the ceremony known as afternoon tea."

—Henry James, *The Portrait of a Lady*

And yet we've swapped it out for dreary Starbucks runs.

TEPEES A roomier alternative to camping tents; I hate stooping.

TELEGRAMS So much chicer than an instant message, and they become great keepsakes and *objets d'art*. A great friend of mine has an infinitely covetable collection of pithy, witty telegrams from Cole Porter to various luminaries.

TELEPHONE BOOKS Both the White Pages and the Yellow Pages make for surprisingly interesting reading. You come across the most astonishing names and get to imagine the astonishing lives that go along with them.

TENNIS WHITES Even though we've entered into a powerhouse era of brute strength, tennis is still at heart an elegant game. Wearing crisp, respectful whites honors that elegance, and does nothing to diminish a player's prowess.

THEMED ROOMS Having a house with the usual bits and bobs ("living room," "dining room," "master bedroom," etc.) is dull, dull, dull. As Diana Vreeland once said: "Never fear being vulgar—just boring." Following her own advice, she and her interior designer created a "Garden in Hell" living room: Persian-flower-covered scarlet chintz swathed the walls and windows; poppy-colored carpeting spilled from the living room into the hallway; red upholstered furniture lurked at every turn.

These other famous themed rooms may inspire you to create your own:

- • • Pauline de Rothchild's French blue library
- • • The ravishing Chinese Room in Britain's Claydon House
- • • James Abbott McNeill Whistler's Peacock Room

THICK WALLS As opposed to the grade-D cardboard that makes up the walls of so many apartment buildings today.

THREE-PIECE SUITS On men, the vest of a three-piece suit somehow contrives to make a rotund stomach look endearing. On women, they just look *sharp* and should therefore mince straight back into our closets.

TIARAS FOR ROYALTY Royals are figureheads, and it depresses me to see them slouching around in jeans.

TIC TACS Happily featured in Wes Anderson's *The Royal Tenenbaums*; the orange ones were given their due in *Juno*. Yet Tic Tacs are hardly enjoying the ubiquity they once enjoyed. Too bad: They always produced such a comforting rattle in one's handbag.

TIMELESSNESS

Playing the piano is a place for me.
Somewhere where time seems to swallow the time that lives in your watch.
The notes, springing from the unborn phrases you are about to hear.
All time, lodged in these stripes of black and white.
I long to bring this place back, and play towards the beginning I haven't heard.

— *Cassie Yukawa* • CONCERT PIANIST

TIN LUNCH BOXES With matching thermoses. Good for clobbering bullies who pester you on the way to school.

TIPSY PARSON An old-fashioned, delicious dessert that consists of several layers of sponge cake absolutely polluted with wine or brandy; this concoction is then sprinkled with almonds and layered with custard. According to one food history Web site, the cake was called "Tipsy Parson" in honor of all the preachers it managed to intoxicate during Sunday home visits.

TOGAS For days when you forget to pick up your dry cleaning; just raid the linen closet.

TOP HATS FOR FORMAL OCCASIONS Especially at presidential inaugurations. Go back and look at old photographs of incoming presidents in their inaugural top hats: They look terribly refined and important.

TWENTIETH-CENTURY PRESIDENTS WHO DONNED TOP HATS
AT THEIR INAUGURAL FESTIVITIES:

fig. 30: YOUR
PRESENCE IS
REQUESTED

Theodore Roosevelt	Herbert Hoover
William H. Taft	Franklin D. Roosevelt
Woodrow Wilson	Harry S. Truman
Warren G. Harding	John F. Kennedy
Calvin Coolidge	

TWENTIETH-CENTURY PRESIDENTS WHO DID NOT:

Dwight Eisenhower	Ronald Reagan
Lyndon Johnson	George H. W. Bush
Richard Nixon	William J. Clinton
Gerald Ford	George W. Bush
James Carter	Barack H. Obama

TOPS They make the most distinctive hum when they're spinning quickly: as unique as the sound of a finger running around the rim of a glass.

TOUPEES There's nothing more delightful than a bad-toupee sighting; Rogaine and hair plugs are making such sightings too scarce these days.

TOWN AND COUNTRY As in: a foothold in each. An enlightened, previously widespread, humane lifestyle that got left behind with other elegances. The compromise of suburbia rarely gives its inhabitants—or their visitors—the satisfaction of either town *or* country.

TOWN CRIERS The original Google alert.

TOWN SQUARES For centuries in Europe, old town squares have served as gathering places for all generations at once, even late at night. Very few contemporary American spaces offer that opportunity today.

TOY SOLDIERS The tin ones with beautifully painted uniforms look so pretty and peaceful: They are more of a style statement than an emblem of violence.

TRADITIONAL ANNIVERSARY GIFTS It is a *very* bad idea to get lazy about giving creative anniversary gifts; Hallmark is *not* an appropriate crutch on which to lean. A list of traditional gifts for significant anniversaries:

- • • **FIRST ANNIVERSARY:** *paper*
- • • **SECOND ANNIVERSARY:** *cotton*
- • • **THIRD ANNIVERSARY:** *leather*
- • • **FIFTH ANNIVERSARY:** *wood*
- • • **TENTH ANNIVERSARY:** *tin, aluminum*
- • • **TWENTIETH ANNIVERSARY:** *china*
- • • **TWENTY-FIFTH ANNIVERSARY:** *silver*
- • • **FIFTIETH ANNIVERSARY:** *gold*
- • • **SIXTIETH ANNIVERSARY:** *diamond*

Start from here and come up with some out-of-the-box interpretations. Opt for fourth-anniversary (some sources say twelfth) silk in this way: Go parachuting together. Nothing is more celebratory than the sight of red parachute silk against a blue sky. For twentieth-anniversary china: Why not take this gift literally and book an adventure for two to Shanghai?

TEXT CONTINUES NEXT PAGE ⟫→

Not everyone knows about this additional flourish, but in England, you can ask Buckingham Palace for a congratulatory message from the Queen commemorating your sixtieth, sixty-fifth, and seventieth wedding anniversary. Apparently in America you can get similar congratulations from the White House on your fiftieth anniversary (which can be quite a bummer if your fiftieth takes place during a presidency that you despise).

TRAGEDIENNES America's young female actresses are encouraged to be so sunny and accessible and sweet these days; this whole girl-next-door cutie-pie business is a bore. If we have to suffer such fools, we should at least get to have their counterpoints as well: Let's bring back good old-fashioned tragediennes (i.e., actresses who specialize in the art of portraying tragedy). Many consider French actress Sarah Bernhardt (1844–1923) to be the greatest tragedienne in the history of the modern stage: She even once played the title role in *Hamlet* in 1899 — a bold experiment at the time.

See also FEMMES FATALES

TRANSATLANTIC CROSSINGS Not to be confused with modern, Disneyfied cruises. Let's bring back those divinely opulent, behemoth, Golden-Age-of-Ocean-Travel, New-York-to-Liverpool liners and all that comes with them: bon voyage parties, cabin-warming parties, flowers sent to cabins, black-tie dinners, invitations to sit at the captain's table, and ballroom dancing.

If you need inspiration on this point, some of the most glamorous and amusing transatlantic cruise films are:

> *Shall We Dance* (1937) with Fred Astaire and Ginger Rogers
> *An Affair to Remember* (1957) with Cary Grant and Deborah Kerr
> *A Night at the Opera* (1935) with the Marx Brothers
> *Gentlemen Prefer Blondes* (1953) with Marilyn Monroe
> *Sabrina* (1954) with Audrey Hepburn
> *The Lady Eve* (1941) with Barbara Stanwyck and Henry Fonda

TRAP DOORS Your colleagues will be *far* less likely to pester you if you have one by your desk.

The most famous American trap doors once lurked in San Francisco's Barbary Coast, which can politely be described as a late-nineteenth-century red-light district. Notorious for its prostitution, gambling, general debauchery, and "Murderer's Alley," the area also featured hidden trapdoors to shanghai dim or drunk sailors when there was a shortage of deckhands; the next morning they would find themselves on a strange ship heading for a faraway port. These features, along with the rest of the Barbary Coast's architecture, were largely destroyed in the 1906 earthquake.

TRAVELING CIRCUSES The sort that travel in magnificent caravans: lions roaring in one wagon; bears growling in another; stilts and feathers and fanfare. Early circuses used to travel with a little orchestra to accompany the daring acts. All of which should, of course, unfold under the traditional bold red-and-white-striped big top.

TREE HOUSES Affordable country homes.

TREE SWINGS Made from rope and boards, tree swings are especially beautiful when ivy is trained down the ropes from the branches above.

In earlier eras, swings were a symbol of sexuality when they appeared in art. Take, for example, the famed rococo oil painting *L'Escarpolette* (French for "The Swing"), painted circa 1766 by Jean-Honoré Fragonard. A swinging woman swathed in a billowing pink gown soars above a young man, who peers up her skirts; another man pushes her from behind. One of the woman's slippers is flying from her extended foot, a gesture sometimes interpreted as a symbol for the loss of virginity. To many observers, this painting came to embody the perceived hedonistic values of the French *ancien régime* on the eve of that country's revolution.

TRAP DOORS

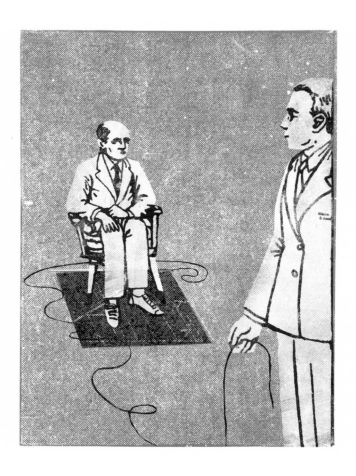

[PLATE 17]

Look out below

TROUSSEAUX A bride of means used to take into her new marriage a *trousseau*, a new wardrobe that befitted her new status in society. For many, it was an excuse for a major shopping splurge; trousseaux were often imported from important couturiers in Paris. Why not nix the expensive wedding, go to City Hall, and blow the wedding budget on glamorous honeymoon clothes instead?

TRUNKS IN ATTICS Mysterious ones that contain old pearls and letters and all sorts of scandalous family secrets.

TULA FURNITURE Adored by wealthy eighteenth-century Russians, Tula tables were made from cut steel; this might sound very industrial, but the surfaces were intricately chiseled to resemble sparkling diamonds — rather like making riches from rags.

"TUNNY" I've seen this word used in cookbooks well into the 1960s; I wonder how "tunny" came to be known exclusively as "tuna," a rather lumpy word in comparison. It seems much sweeter to give a child a sandwich filled with "tunny" than "tuna."

TURBANS In early-twentieth-century Western fashion, they evolved as a cheap and chic alternative to expensive, elaborate hats. Wrapping a bit of jersey around your head, turban-style, is the fastest way to deal with a bad hair day *and* transport yourself to 1920s Paris at the same time.

Prada recently revived the turban, but the trend seemed stillborn in the mass market; these new, brightly hued satin versions towered a little too high in the front and looked costumey. Volume-wise, it might be best to tread lightly when it comes to today's turbans, lest the wearer invite unfortunate comparisons to *Sunset Boulevard*'s campy Norma Desmond, or Rosie the Riveter.

TURRETS Just imagine the amount of writing a girl could get done in one: Turrets are truly "a room of one's own."

TUTTI-FRUTTI I first came across fruit-filled tutti-frutti in Truman Capote's 1948 short story, "Children on Their Birthdays," in which it is indeed being served as a birthday treat; Capote always manages to make such confections sound charming and absolutely hallowed.

Here is a 1906 recipe for tutti-frutti ice cream, from *Recipes from the Inglenook Cookbook by the Sisters of the Brethren Church*:

TUTTI-FRUTTI

To 2 quarts of rich cream add 1 pound of pulverized sugar and 4 eggs well beaten; mix together well, then place on the fire, stirring constantly until brought to the boiling point. Remove immediately and continue to stir until cold. Add vanilla to taste, place in a freezer and when about half frozen mix thoroughly into it 1 pound of preserved fruits in equal parts of peaches, cherries, pineapple, orange, banana, etc. All these fruits are to be cut into small pieces and mixed well with the frozen cream. Mix a color in this, so it will be in veins like marble.

This recipe, submitted by Sister Rose E. Smith of Dunlap, Kansas, also included some rather surprising instructions for "molding the cream"; she advises you to "sprinkle with a little carmine dissolved in a little water with 2 drops of spirits of ammonia."

TYPEWRITERS The print from a typewriter can be as personalized as handwriting, an extension of one's writerly persona; this is certainly not something you can say about a Times New Roman printout from your computer.

A LIST OF THE PREFERRED TYPEWRITERS OF A FEW FAMOUS WRITERS:

• • • **JACK KEROUAC:** *Underwood early 1930s portable, Royal Standard*
• • • **ISAK DINESEN** (a.k.a. Karen Blixen): *1918 Corona No. 3*
• • • **ERNEST HEMINGWAY:** *Coronas No. 3 and No. 4, Underwood Noiseless Portable, various Royal portables, Halda Portable*
• • • **PAUL AUSTER:** *Olympia SM 9*
• • • **WILLIAM FAULKNER:** *Underwood Standard Portable, Remington Model 12, Olympia SM-1*
• • • **ERNIE PYLE:** *Corona No. 3 Portable*
• • • **ROBERT LOUIS STEVENSON:** *Hammond*

fig. 31: THE CORONA NO. 3: ALL THE RAGE IN 1912

UFO SIGHTINGS They seem to be waning in popularity; perhaps they are the domain of a more outdoors-oriented culture than ours currently is.

UMBRELLAS Beautiful ones with carved handles, instead of those silly guaranteed-to-break-immediately quasi-disposable ones that you always see jutting out of street-corner garbage cans. After all, as writer Robert Louis Stevenson once wrote in an essay titled "The Philosophy of Umbrellas":

> A ribbon of the Legion of Honour or a string of medals may prove a person's courage; a title may prove his birth; a professorial chair his study and acquirement; but it is the habitual carriage of the umbrella that is the stamp of Respectability. The umbrella has become the acknowledged index of social position.

"UNDERDRAWERS" I don't know why this word conjures up such a funny image, but it does.

fig. 32: GIMME SHELTER

UNFINISHED CASTLES BY ECCENTRIC GENIUSES Sometimes an unfinished palace is a thousand times more memorable than the finished product would have been. Everyone is familiar with the unfinished castles of "Mad" King Ludwig II of Bavaria, but there are many more such structures throughout the world, including:

LA SAGRADA FAMILIA (BARCELONA, SPAIN)

Work on this fantastical cathedral began in 1882; its architect, Antoni Gaudí, died in 1926 without seeing its completion. In fact, it is *still* being built and the construction is likely to continue until "some time in the first third of the 21st century," according to the cathedral's official Web site. Tile-mosaic statues of yellow, orange, purple, and green fruits are heaped on top of the church's spires; Gaudí had intended for the entire facade to be vividly colored, although authorities say that this costly vision is unlikely to be realized.

TEXT CONTINUES NEXT PAGE ⟫⟶

LA CUESTA ENCANTADA (SAN SIMEON, CALIFORNIA)

High on a hill overlooking the Pacific Ocean, William Randolph Hearst began construction on La Cuesta Encantada ("The Enchanted Hill") in 1919 and continued for nearly thirty years. The compound included:

- • • Hearst's own 165-room mansion
- • • A series of guesthouse mini-mansions
- • • Ancient Rome–inspired indoor and outdoor pools
- • • An exotic tree orchard
- • • The world's largest personal zoo
- • • An airstrip, which welcomed the planes of some of the world's most famous aviators, including Howard Hughes, Amelia Earhart, and Charles Lindbergh

Yet La Cuesta Encantada was never finished. According to one guidebook, the warehouses at San Simeon contain packing crates still stuffed with European treasures, stripped from overseas palaces and monasteries and sent to California to furnish Hearst's castle. This sprawling Monument to Ego was immortalized as "Xanadu" in Orson Welles's classic film, *Citizen Kane.*

LONGWOOD (NATCHEZ, MISSISSIPPI)

This plantation mansion is also known as "Nutt's Folly" in honor of its owner and creator, Dr. Haller Nutt. Designed to be an octagonal Oriental Revival showcase (complete with an onion dome) amid a sea of Greek Revival planters' palaces, Longwood's construction began in 1860. The work was largely done by Yankee workers; when the Civil War broke out, the workers abandoned the construction and went back north to enlist. If you visit Longwood today, the workers' tools are right where they left them, covered by decades-old layers of dirt and dust. Of the thirty-two planned rooms, only nine were completed. After the war, the newly impoverished Nutt family dwelled in Longwood's basement with the remnants of their fine furniture, plaster falling on them from the ceilings above, and the skeleton of the unfinished palace creaking above their heads.

An amusing side note about King Ludwig: In her colorful memoir, *D.V.*, Diana Vreeland describes the fêtes once hosted by the deeply peculiar royal at Linderhof palace, in which the illustrious guests were a series of marble busts. Sometimes the bust of Louis XIV would join Ludwig at the dining room table; at other times, the busts of Madame de Maintenon or Madame de Pompadour would be on hand to make charming conversation during the meal. The food-laden table came up through a hole in the floor so "that *they* never had to see a servant."

UPSIDE-DOWN LOCKS A nineteenth-century superstitious interior design flourish used in the South, as a way to trick ghosts who might be trying to enter a locked bedroom.

UTOPIA The pursuit thereof. A perfectly just society is always a worthy goal.

V_{plus}W

VALUING PERSONAL PRIVACY OVER PUBLICITY

Let's revive the sense that some personal matters are no one else's business—not the government's, or commercial marketers', or the media's. Nowadays, everything that we do, say, read, or even think is treated as public property, to be recorded, disseminated, and retained in easily accessible databases. Worse yet, this reduction in the personal privacy we enjoy as a factual reality also reduces the legal protection we enjoy as privacy rights. That's because the Supreme Court has held that the Constitution's privacy protection extends only to expectations of privacy that society considers "reasonable." Therefore, the less value our society places on privacy, the less protection the courts give to it, precipitating a downward spiral.

George Orwell's classic dystopia, *1984* (published in 1949), powerfully depicted the dehumanizing, degrading impact of merely knowing that "Big Brother is watching"—even without any violence or repression. In contrast, too many members of our show-all, tell-all, publicity-craving culture ask, "So what? Why should I care who's watching, since I have nothing to hide?" Vanishing is the sense that even—indeed, especially— those of us who have committed no crimes or other acts that we want to hide because they are shameful, still would seek to hide our personal thoughts and beliefs, our intimate actions and interactions. Personal privacy fosters the flourishing of our individual personalities and intimate relationships.

—*Nadine Strossen* • PROFESSOR OF LAW, NEW YORK LAW SCHOOL; FORMER PRESIDENT, AMERICAN CIVIL LIBERTIES UNION

VANITY TABLES New York grande dame Nan Kempner used to say that the best part of a party was getting ready. Vanity tables make that ritual much more luxurious, much more so than raking on makeup in front of a bathroom mirror.

VEILS Veils belong at funerals as well as weddings: They are a now-lost visual symbol of profound loss. They lend a respectful gravitas to the ceremony and also preserve the privacy of the bereaved widow. It's unlikely that anyone will ever forget the image of Jacqueline Kennedy's simple black veil at her husband's funeral.

VICES I'd rather be Scarlett O'Hara than Melanie Wilkes *any* day of the week.

fig. 33: WOEFUL ARE *the* VICE-LESS

VICTORIAN GRASS Sometimes, the grass actually *is* greener on the other side of the fence. In the 1800s, when the perfecting of lawns was a deadly serious pursuit, Victorians paid special attention to the soil bed beneath the grass, cultivating it as deeply as a foot and a half (modern lawns, by comparison, are usually sown in only an inch or two of soil). Apparently this practice allows the lawn to root very deeply and draw on reserves of moisture and nutrients in times of drought or duress; it also supposedly made Victorian grass a deep, gorgeous *emerald* green not seen today.

VIONNET, MADELEINE (1876–1975) An iconic 1920s and '30s French designer, Vionnet is regarded by many experts as the greatest dressmaker of the twentieth century. She took a deeply architectural and intellectual approach to her creations and is perhaps most famous for her famed "hand-kerchief dress," which consisted of squares of silk assembled on a then-revolutionary bias cut, which Vionnet herself pioneered. These dresses clung sensuously to the curves of their (often-famous) wearers and left abso-lutely *nothing* to the imagination—an intensely daring notion in that era.

TEXT CONTINUES NEXT PAGE ⟫⟫⟫→

Vionnet's peer Coco Chanel is often credited with emancipating women from corseted clothing and silhouettes, but a whole host of Chanel's contemporaries and predecessors deserve to share this credit—particularly Vionnet, who rejected any padding or constructions that would interfere with the natural form. She even used barefoot models to present her first solo collection, which would be considered somewhat avant-garde even today (not to mention a relief to contemporary runway models, who've lately been falling smack off their stiletto platforms).

VREELAND, DIANA (C. 1906–1989) It's hard to know where to begin or end when it comes to the great Diana Vreeland: She was a rare, remarkable figure who made life seem less linear.

Vreeland helmed American *Vogue* from 1962 to 1971; like her eventual successor, Anna Wintour, Vreeland was bathed in the national spotlight during her tenure at the magazine. She appeared in fictionalized form in the 1957 film *Funny Face* as Maggie Prescott, the amusingly dictatorial and emphatic editor of *Quality* magazine. Maggie's signature exclamation—"Let's give 'em the old *pizzazz*!"—sounded remarkably like Vreeland on any given day at the office.

Famous for her *bon mots* and fantastical, bold gestures, Vreeland was the perfect Space Age fashion editor, constantly challenging the industry to cross new frontiers. She encouraged women to never fear being vulgar, only boring—advice that she most *certainly* followed herself. Vreeland's very appearance reflected her mantra that beauty could sometimes be strange and even alarming: patent-black hair; long red-lacquered talons; a severely painted red mouth, and sometimes even rouged *earlobes*. Every morning, her maid ironed her money and polished her shoes—top *and* bottom.

Vreeland never let the boring old truth interfere with her self-perception or the image of herself that she projected to the world; a mix of fact and fiction ("faction," she called it) was her preferred *modus operandi*. According to Vreeland, throughout the course of her life, she had:

- • • Sat in the rafters at King George's coronation;
- • • Befriended "Buffalo" Bill Cody on a childhood excursion to Wyoming;
- • • Witnessed the Lindbergh flight while sitting on her suburban lawn with her husband's bootlegger;

- • • Sat with Josephine Baker and her diamond-collared cheetah in the balconies of a Paris movie house;
- • • Got into a fistfight of sorts with überagent Swifty Lazar at a dinner party given by the Oscar de la Rentas.

There are countless similar Vreeland anecdotes. While some of her literal-minded contemporaries scoffed at her tenuous relationship with reality, they *totally* missed the point, which was always about making an impression, creating a unique *world*. As Vreeland said in *D.V.*:

> Did I tell you about the zebras lining the driveway at San Simeon? You believed that, didn't you? Did I tell you that Lindbergh flew over Brewster? It could have been someone else, but who cares—*fake it!* . . . There's only one thing in life, and that's the continual renewal of inspiration.

VW BUGS The 1970s sort, like the one Annie Hall tears around in. The opposite of midlife-crisis cars like Porsches, those VWs were zippy, stylish, and amusingly self-deprecating.

WALKING, THE ART OF Or "walking well," as Christian Dior put it. Sadly, today it's regarded as just another lost finishing school art.

WALKING DINNERS A boisterous old-time Southern take on the potluck supper, in which a single dinner party would be given at several different houses. You would have drinks at one home (juleps on the front porch, likely), and then walk to the next for appetizers. The main course would follow in yet another hostess's dining room, and then everyone would stagger to their final destination for dessert, brandy, and cigars.

WALK-IN FIREPLACES Not that you ever really *need* to walk into a fireplace, but they are very dramatic regardless.

WALLPAPERED CARS On the *inside*, not the outside, of course. This hasn't really been done since the 1920s and '30s, when people rode around in those fine big boxy "horseless carriages"; the passenger compartments of these vehicles often bore neat little wall patterns. Reviving the trend might be a nice touch for people who practically live in their automobiles, such as Los Angelenos.

WAMPUM These beads made from purple-hued shells—once used as a currency of exchange between the early colonists and some East Coast Native American tribes—would still make a very satisfying form of money. I like the idea of carrying around a velvet sack filled with clacking shells, instead of another boring old leather wallet.

WARDIAN CASES It's a great shame that whimsical Wardian cases—also known as terrariums—are rarely found in our houses today. My grandparents had a fauna-filled one, and as a little girl I peered into it for hours, probably looking for fairies or some such. Glass Wardian cases were extremely popular in upscale Victorian homes: filled with prized ferns, orchids, and other flowers, these pretty miniature greenhouses sat proudly on tables or on elaborately wrought stands.

Equally adored by the Victorians were the following indoor-flora decorations:

- • • **WINDOW GARDENS,** which consisted of elaborately staged plant landscapes in an oversize bay window. To the Victorian eye, windows and balconies looked positively empty if not heaving with foliage, "climbers," and bold flowers. Sometimes glass doors were even affixed to the bay windows to seal the flowers off, creating a greenhouse of sorts and protecting the precious plants from gas (still used for lights) and insects.

- • • **IVY-FRAMED MIRRORS,** which were another favorite parlor item: all four sides of a mirror were draped in live ivy; the plant's pot was attached to the back of the mirror.

- • • **IVY SCREENS,** which were simply large, freestanding screens covered in live ivy; they made functional *objets d'art* and were used in drawing rooms as room dividers.

- • • **PARLOR BOWERS:** large, domed, ivy- or leaf-covered arbors under which love seats were placed.

[PLATE 18]

Like no other

WASP WAISTS This nineteenth-century fashion silhouette featured a drastically cinched waist; the result made a woman's body look segmented, like a wasp's body. It's best to relegate those dangerously corseted looks to the past, but a gentle variation—which implicitly highlights and celebrates a woman's natural curves—would be most attractive.

WATER MILLS The sound of rushing water must be very soothing to hear at night.

WATERMELON FRUIT BASKETS In which watermelons are carved into handled baskets and filled with fruit salad; they are very festive for picnics and carry with them a hint of whimsical resourcefulness.

WAX LIPS Other old-guard candy like this should stage a simultaneous comeback: wax fangs, wax moustaches, wax cola bottles, candy cigarettes, chocolate or bubblegum cigars, candy necklaces, Atomic Fireballs, Pop Rocks ("Entertainment for your whole mouth!"), Fun Dip (with the two "Lik-A-Stix" candy spatulas), and Pixy Stix (which are like legal crack).

See also FAKE VOMIT

"WELL, I NEVER" A good, old-fangled response to hearing surprising information, usually in a gossip scenario. A wonderful alternative to the popularly exclaimed reactive phrase, "Shut up!" or "No way."

WEST, MAE (1893–1980) Old Hollywood's Queen of Sassy One-Liners; so sassy, in fact, that West was banned from NBC Radio after a scandalous, double-entendre-laden guest appearance in 1937. Many young people today would recognize her famous quips but are less likely to be familiar with the woman who uttered them:

- • • "I used to be Snow White, but I drifted."
- • • "Too much of a good thing can be wonderful."
- • • "A hard man is good to find."
- • • "When I'm good, I'm very good—but when I'm bad, I'm better."

- • • "Good girls go to heaven. Bad girls go everywhere else."
- • • "When women go wrong, men go right after them."
- • • "I've been in more laps than a napkin."

West was not just famous for her outrageous wit: Nearly every part of her curvaceous physique was immortalized by some aspect of international pop culture:

- • • The Coca-Cola bottle's design was said to have been inspired by her body.
- • • The "Mae West Lips Sofa," created by Surrealist Salvador Dalí in 1937, remains one of the artist's most recognizable works.
- • • Her torso was immortalized in the body-shaped bottle of Elsa Schiaparelli's best-selling Shocking! perfume.
- • • World War II–era inflatable life vests were named as an homage to her pillowy bosom (the term "Mae West" for a life jacket apparently continues to this day).

West hardly protested such objectification; as she once reportedly said, "I didn't discover curves; I only uncovered them."

WET NURSES Breastfeeding one's own children is seriously in fashion today; still, it would be nice to have the option. Imagine: a happily breast-fed child, and you get your pretty small breasts back. It's the best of all worlds.

WHARTON, EDITH (1862–1937) As in, let's bring her back in her appropriate context. These days, any time some vapid author writes some vapid novel about vapid wealthy people flouncing about New York City, it is described as "Whartonian." The phrase is as abused as the label "genius." I'm willing to bet that the people describing such works in this manner have never read a single paragraph of Wharton's ingenious, nuanced works.

"WHIPPERSNAPPER" A perfectly wonderful word from the late 1600s, meaning "an unimportant but offensively presumptuous person, especially a young one." We certainly still have plenty of such creatures around today; why not revive this amusingly insulting term for them?

WHIRLIGIG PUNCH A whirligig is an object that spins or whirls; I guess the idea behind the name is that this punch will leave your head spinning. Have a gander at this 1920s recipe and you'll see why:

WHIRLIGIG PUNCH

1 bottle champagne
1 jigger cognac
2 jiggers sherry
3 dashes Curaçao
3 dashes maraschino
2 teaspoons confectioners' sugar
1 slice fresh cubed pineapple
½ orange, sliced, with skin and membrane removed
2 slices fresh pear
Berries
Sprigs of mint for garnish

Mix all of the ingredients except mint in a large pitcher with ice. Garnish with mint sprigs and serve immediately, in champagne goblets.

WHISPERING CHAIRS These stylish, domed-topped chairs must have been designed with either gossiping females or spies in mind: They make it practically impossible to be casually overheard except by the person sitting directly across from you. If you want a wonderful treat, go to BG Restaurant in New York City's Bergdorf Goodman; ask for tea table with the butter-colored yellow whispering chairs overlooking Fifth Avenue and Central Park; this is one of the most special views in the city, from one of the most special perches.

WHISTLING It's strange that in today's culture of extroversion, we seem to have grown too self-conscious to whistle while walking down the street.

WHITE CAST-IRON LAWN FURNITURE It's not terribly comfortable, but that's beside the point. White-iron lawn furniture looks very elegant and crisp against the green of a lawn: It's the perfect place to eat macaroons and write letters with scented ink.

WHITE GLOVES AND PARTY MANNERS

White Gloves and Party Manners (1965) was my bedtime story growing up; this yellow-covered etiquette book featured subjects such as "Telephone Manners," "How to Act with Grownups," "The Fine Young Art of Conversation," and "Good Grooming Can Be Fun." At the time, I would roll my eyes and make fun of my mother as she tried to teach manners to my sisters, brother, and me. Now as an adult, I am so thankful for my mother's lessons: Manners not only teach you to feel comfortable in any social situation, but, most important, they teach you how to make others feel welcome and comfortable. Just think: If everyone in the world felt welcome, wouldn't it be a more beautiful place?

—*Janie Bryant* • COSTUME DESIGNER, *MAD MEN*

WHITE PANTSUITS FOR WOMEN They've been coming in and out of fashion for decades: Worn with a straw fedora or boater hat, beautifully tailored white pantsuits can look as light and breezy as summer itself. Marlene Dietrich—a pioneer of the Victor/Victoria look—sometimes used to wear white tails for her stage finales.

WHITE NURSE UNIFORMS With those matching little hats: sick people deserve something stylish to look at, especially in hospitals.

WHITE PICKET FENCES Somewhere along the line, they became the symbol of a deeply conventional suburban existence—which is too bad, because they can give a crisp facelift to a property in any setting. As famed interior designer Elsie de Wolfe used to say, great feats can be accomplished with white paint.

WHITE TENNIS BALLS AT WIMBLEDON This major tennis tournament requires players to don all-white court garb, but long gone are the white tennis balls once used in the matches, which must have looked very pretty against the green grass courts.

"WHORE'S BATHS" As Holly Golightly said about her lover, José, in the novella *Breakfast at Tiffany's*: "He takes about fifty baths a day: men ought to smell *some*what." Americans are very sanitary creatures; our shower-twice-a-day culture is so time-consuming. Holly's right: Both men *and* women should occasionally get away with smelling *some*what. The luridly named whore's bath is a good sometime-solution: A quick dousing of one's pits and parts, or a mere spritz of cologne or perfume to refresh the senses, and you're ready to go.

WICKER BABY CARRIAGES After all, babyhood is one of the few times we can get away with unabashed quaintness. Today's baby transportation is starting to look outright sci-fi: Those creepy baby-carriage tripods whirl around the supermarket, as though by remote control. Who wants to begin life as an extra on the set of *Alien*?

fig. 34: THE PERAMBULATO

WICKER BASKETS ON BICYCLES They look best filled with freshly cut flowers and other farmers'-market goodies.

WIDE-LEGGED PANTS Both stylish *and* merciful to the wearer: one of the few fashionable items of clothing that can make this claim. The diametrically opposite, ironically named "skinny jeans" that editors and retailers have been peddling during the last few years can make even the slenderest figure look like a fat inverted triangle—especially when combined with flats.

WIDOW'S WALKS The wives of sea captains and sailors would pace these rooftop platforms when their men were out on voyages, and watch for the ship's return each night. Yet the sailors often perished at sea, and hence the term "widow's walk" came about. The older houses of Nantucket Island — the whaling capital of the world in the early 1800s — sport a beautiful array of widow's walks. Just walk up the residential end of Main Street and survey the roofs of the historic homes there. Some of the enclosed ones still have the original wavy paned glass in the windows. One gets the sense that those old widows are still pacing there each night, centuries later.

WIGWAMS Easier to build than hobbit holes, and just as fanciful and cozy.

WIMPLES ON NUNS They're so imposing. Old nuns especially *should* look imposing. It's their *job*.

WIND-UP PHONOGRAPH PLAYERS The very old ones with magnificent, trumpet flower–like amplifiers: the best way to listen to recordings of songs such as "Top Hat, White Tie and Tails" and "Cheek to Cheek." Tilt the amplifier away from the machine and affix a short flickering candle to the center of the record, where it will spin around gently in time to the music.

WINTER PICNICS Icy champagne + snow = new levels of revelation.

"WISECRACKS" And of course, the word "wisecracker."

WISHING WELLS There should be one per square mile.

WITS Wits are curious creatures: Although solitary at heart, they are often known to rove about in packs. Case in point: Dorothy Parker and the cruel wits of the famed Algonquin Round Table, of which Parker was the undisputed queen. This delicious viper nest of writers, critics, and other blade-tongued individuals met daily for a barb-fest luncheon at New York City's Algonquin Hotel, at which wit was the currency. You always had to be on your toes, or you were bled in full view of the others. Parker herself *never* disappointed. For example, once during a word game, Parker was asked to use the word "horticulture" in a sentence. Without missing a beat, Parker responded: "You can lead a horticulture, but you can't make her think."

On the other side of the Atlantic, playwright Oscar Wilde had long cornered the market on wit; his *bons mots* were often tinged with hilarious misanthropy:

- • • "A man's face is his autobiography. A woman's face is her work of fiction."
- • • "Relations are simply a tedious pack of people, who haven't got the remotest knowledge of how to live, nor the smallest instinct about when to die."
- • • "One's real life is so often the life that one does not lead."
- • • "A true friend stabs you in the front."
- • • "Biography lends to death a new terror."

WITCH HAZEL Nearly every woman in America used to have a *jug* of witch hazel in her bathroom. Besides having a perfectly delightful name, this potion is supposed to tame bruises and soothe acne; mollify shaving nicks, mosquito bites, and other cuts; treat ingrown toenails and—when squirted on cotton pads and placed on eyes—reduce bags in about two seconds. Why it exited our cupboards I will never know.

WOOD-BURNING FIREPLACES Those clinical gas ones that you turn on via a switch on the wall are about as cheery as a blowtorch.

[PLATE 19]

with friends like these

WOOLLCOTT, ALEXANDER (1887–1943) This king of the famed Algonquin Round Table proves the saying that fact is often stranger than fiction: As a character in a book, Woollcott would have been simply too outlandish to be believed. A vicious drama critic for the *New York Times,* Woollcott swathed his 250-pound body in swirling opera capes with poppy-red linings; he often welcomed friends to the lunch table with greetings such as "Hello, repulsive." I wish we could bottle him up and use him as a sort of social mace.

WORDPLAY An underfunded and underacknowledged art.

WORTH, CHARLES FREDERICK (1825–1895) The father of French haute couture was ironically an Englishman—a Mr. Charles Worth, who opened his shop in Paris on the Rue de la Paix in 1858. The *bon ton* of his day reportedly had Mr. Worth to thank for introducing the bustle, hoop skirt, designer label, and live models (who, according to Vanity Fair, were selected "not for their beauty but for their resemblances to his best customers"). Empress Eugénie, Napoleon III's wife, touted Worth's designs—made from dramatic fabrics and extravagant trimmings—making him the era's most sought-after artisanal dressmaker.

Before long, clients from all around the world traveled to Paris to purchase entire wardrobes from the House of Worth. According to the Metropolitan Museum of Art, "a complete wardrobe would consist of morning, after-noon, and evening dresses and lavish 'undress' items such as tea gowns and nightgowns, which were worn only in the privacy of one's home." Worth also provided society belles and grande dames with sumptuous wedding and masquerade ball gowns. Worth clothing became such an international symbol of luxury that many American women—always more susceptible to Puritanical guilt than their decadent European sisters—would stash away their newly acquired Worth dresses for a couple of years before wearing them. This gesture showed that they were, after all, only partial slaves to fashion. The House of Worth had an excellent hundred-year dynastic run, closing in 1952 with the retirement of Worth's great-grandson, Jean-Charles.

A side note: Only two American designers have ever been officially classi-fied as haute couturiers in France: Main Rousseau Bocher (also known as "Mainbocher") and Ralph Rucci, a contributor to this book.

See also HUMILITY

THE WPA Let's not just invest in crumbling banks; let's invest, FDR-style, in our nation's strained infrastructure. Created by the government during the Depression, the Works Progress Administration created millions of jobs nationwide. According to Jim F. Couch, coauthor of *The Political Economy of the New Deal,* "almost every community in America has a park, bridge, or school constructed by the agency." As of 1940, the WPA had built:

- • • 4,383 new school buildings and made repairs and additions to more than 30,000 others
- • • More than 130 hospitals; improvements were made to another 1,670
- • • Nearly 9,000 miles of new storm drains and sanitary sewer lines

The agency planted 24 million trees and built or refurbished more than 2,500 sports stadiums around the country. This sounds like a better investment than handing over tax dollars to pad corporate bonuses.

WRIST CHANGE PURSES The prettiest ones were hidden underneath a cloth flower; they looked like corsages on a lady's wrist and were just big enough for her taxi money and lipstick.

WORLD-TOUR HONEYMOONS Banish the sluggish, clichéd resort retreat.

X y and Z

"X" MARKS THE SPOT As in: faded old treasure maps that you would improbably find in your grandparents' attics.

YARN HAIR RIBBONS Tied in bows around pigtails, ponytails, and the ends of braids. They always unraveled, but that was part of their charm.

YARNS As in, a "good yarn." A tall tale. An outlandish fib of a story.

YELLOW-BULBED THEATER MARQUEES There's something heady about seeing movie stars' names spelled out in lights, and something distinctly discrediting about seeing those same names in cellophane letters, showcased against a dingy, flickering fluorescent backdrop.

THE YELLOW BOOK First published in London in 1894, *The Yellow Book* was a notorious avant-garde magazine determined to beam a ray of light into the dusty closet of Victorian literary sensibilities. While it only had a (controversial) three-year run, the publication was the talk of London's salon society; it included the writings of Henry James, William Butler Yeats, and Max Beerbohm and the illustrations of the great Aubrey Beardsley. Wholly dedicated to breaking artistic barriers, *The Yellow Book* shaped the genre of the short story and showcased new and exciting forms of writing. It would be nice if we had a similarly trail-blazing literary publication today; I feel like I read the same short story over and over again in today's prominent fiction-publishing magazines.

See also THE ART OF THIS CENTURY GALLERY

YELLOW CAFÉ LIGHTS ON STRINGS One of the few forms of electric light that can be as flattering and evocative as candlelight.

THE YULE LOG In the 1960s, television programming was occasionally suspended for a few hours on Christmas Eve; then some genius came up with the idea of replacing a static-filled or black screen with an image of a burning yule log. As a result, viewers who tuned to New York's WPIX on December 24, 1966, were treated to three hours of looped footage of yule logs flaming cheerily away in a fireplace, accompanied by Christmas music.

Time magazine has called the WPIX Yule Log "a surrealist's joke, a postmodernist's dream—the television, literally, as the family hearth—and an immediate success." Many other stations picked up WPIX's footage or shot their own—but television executives extinguished the flame in 1989, preferring to use the slot for revenue-producing programming instead.

ZEPPELINS The chicest way to travel, aside from the old Orient Express.

THE ZIEGFELD FOLLIES These lavish, wildly creative Broadway revue productions—which ran from 1907 through 1931—are likely most remembered today for the beautiful chorus girls, nicknamed the "Ziegfeld girls"; yet every aspect of the Ziegfeld productions was a feat of imagination and engineering. Founded by showman Florenz Ziegfeld—who sought to "glorify the American Girl"—the legendary Follies has long embodied Broadway at its most glamorous.

Many films have devoted themselves to re-creating the Follies and portraying the lives of its stars and creator; *The Great Ziegfeld* (1936) contains one astonishing scene that captures the extravagance of the original shows: an eight-minute number called "A Pretty Girl Is Like a Melody," one of the most famous musical performances ever filmed. Shot in a single take, the scene centered around a tall, elaborate, revolving set shaped like a wedding cake; on the tops of the spiraling layers danced nearly two hundred elaborately costumed performers in various historical scenarios, including a Viennese ball and an eighteenth-century French court. Elsewhere a "Japanese" princess sings an aria from *Madama Butterfly*, women dressed as masked bats swoop up and down the stairs, along with others dressed as eagle-headed valkyries. In one section of the set, the "floor" is composed of the tops of a dozen or so white pianos, onto which the bat ladies descend and dance.

TEXT CONTINUES NEXT PAGE ⟫→

[PLATE 20]

the marvelous Zeppelin

The total effect of all of this plumage and fanfare is nearly indescribable—but it came at a price: According to one source, the set and shot cost "more than the entire Follies would have set back Ziggie himself in the grand days."

See also MILK BATHS

ZIGGURATS Popular among the Assyrians and Babylonians, these ancient pyramid temples were very chic. Their distinguishing feature: They were usually terraced, making it easy to stop and have a restorative lemonade while climbing to the top in the hot sun.

While largely forgotten by most people, modern architects still occasionally reference the design; for example, the famous Solomon R. Guggenheim Museum in New York was conceived by architect Frank Lloyd Wright as an "inverted ziggurat."

ZINC BARS These traditional Parisian bistros were named for their now-rare zinc-topped bars, which looked terribly modern during the height of their popularity in the early twentieth century. "Zincs" have become an evocative symbol of the 1920s expatriate life (look for their mention in Hemingway's novel *The Sun Also Rises*); the Musée Montmartre in Paris has thoughtfully preserved one as an homage to its role in the lives of the Lost Generation.

The End

cheers TO YOU:

ACKNOWLEDGMENTS

I WOULD LIKE TO THANK MANY INDIVIDUALS for their tireless support; without their help and enthusiasm, my project would not have been possible, and I am very grateful to each of them:

My sage editor at Chronicle Books, Emily Haynes; my irrepressible agent, Kate Lee; my editor at the *Huffington Post* and earliest *Let's Bring Back* cohort, Anya Strzemien; my assistant, Nour Akkad; Willow Bay; Tim Tomkinson; Larissa Silva; Amanda Christine Miller; Michele Wissot; Valeria McColloch; Elissa Lumley; Glynnis MacNicol; Liesl Schillinger; Chase Bodine; Rosina Rucci; Jesse Sheidlower; Dallas Sowers, Monica Macek; Christine Bauch; Bil Donovan; Caitlin Crounse; Frances J. B. McCarthy, Esq.; Jessica Sailer; Melinda Arons; Stephan Wurth; Dora Militaru; Mauri Weakley; Elisabeth Saint-Amand; Alexander Woolfson; James Pavey; David Foote; and Ruth Kligman.

I am particularly indebted to my gracious guest contributors: Jonathan Adler, Leticia Baldrige, Daniel Boulud, James L. Brooks, Janie Bryant, Coralle Charriol Paul, Simon Doonan, Nora Ephron, Arianna Huffington, Ted Koppel, Karl Kozel, Coralie Charriol Paul, Jennifer Lynn Pelka, Ralph Rucci, Lisa Salzer, James Sanders, Kate Spade, Nadine Strossen, Lindy Woodhead, and Cassie Yukawa.

Thank you also to the following institutions: The Costume Institute, Joanne Hendricks Antiquarian Cookbooks, the International Center of Photography, the Metropolitan Museum of Art, the New York Botanical Garden, and New York Vintage.

I would like to offer a separate note of gratitude to my husband, Gregory Macek, who for many months patiently tolerated a chaotic atmosphere of nostalgia as I wrote this book. Although I guess our life together is, to a certain extent, *always* a chaos of nostalgia, so perhaps not that much really changed.

• • •———————————— *Come back soon*